Faith in a Pluralist Age

Faith in a Pluralist Age

EDITED BY
Kaye V. Cook

CASCADE *Books* • Eugene, Oregon

FAITH IN A PLURALIST AGE

Copyright © 2018 Kaye V. Cook. All rights reserved. Except for brief quotations in critical publications or reviews, no part of this book may be reproduced in any manner without prior written permission from the publisher. Write: Permissions, Wipf and Stock Publishers, 199 W. 8th Ave., Suite 3, Eugene, OR 97401.

Cascade Books
An Imprint of Wipf and Stock Publishers
199 W. 8th Ave., Suite 3
Eugene, OR 97401

www.wipfandstock.com

PAPERBACK ISBN: 978-1-5326-0994-7
HARDCOVER ISBN: 978-1-5326-0996-1
EBOOK ISBN: 978-1-5326-0995-4

Cataloguing-in-Publication data:

Names: Cook, Kaye V.
Title: Faith in a pluralist age / Kaye V. Cook.
Description: Eugene, OR: Cascade Books, 2018 | Series: if applicable | Includes bibliographical references and index.
Identifiers: ISBN 978-1-5326-0994-7 (paperback) | ISBN 978-1-5326-0996-1 (hardcover) | ISBN 978-1-5326-0995-4 (ebook)
Subjects: LCSH: subject | subject | subject | subject
Classification: CALL NUMBER 2018 (print) | CALL NUMBER (ebook)

Manufactured in the U.S.A.   MARCH 7, 2018

I dedicate this book to Peter Berger, whose death before its publication robbed the world of an "incurable" Lutheran and preeminent sociologist. His often contrarian thinking has transformed the ways we think about God, culture, and being. Unwilling to join the "God is dead" movement and deny the reality of his own experience, he came instead to challenge the secularization hypothesis, proposing that we live in a pluralist age, not a secularist age. As he so wisely put it, this insight alters the place of religion in our lives and society. The rest, to borrow a phrase that he quotes from Hillel, is commentary.

Table of Contents

Preface, Kaye V. Cook ix
Acknowledgement xvii

Chapter 1: Faith in a Pluralist Age, PETER L. BERGER 1

THEORETICAL RESPONSES

Chapter 2: Christian Sociology between Appreciation, Dissent, Communication, and Contribution, BRUCE C. WEARNE 17

Chapter 3: Maintaining Christian Consistency in a Pluralist Context, ROGER E. OLSON 29

Chapter 4: Faith and Politics in a Pluralist Age, PAUL A. BRINK 37

Chapter 5: Doing Justice to Diverse Ways of Life, JAMES W. SKILLEN 46

PLURALISM IN CULTURAL CONTEXT

Chapter 6: Hindu Nationalism against Religious Pluralism—or, the Sacralization of Religious Identity and Its Discontents in Present-Day India, THOMAS A. HOWARD 62

Chapter 7: Gendered Wrath: Reflections on Anger and Forgiveness, RUTH GROENHOUT 79

Chapter 8: Evangelical Christianity and Women's Roles in Contemporary Brazil: Marginalization or Modernization?, RUTH M. MELKONIAN-HOOVER 90

Chapter 9: The Stranger's Address in Modernizing Cultures: Values and Pluralist Ideas among Brazilian and Chinese Christians, KAYE V. COOK, SI-HUA CHANG, AND TAYLOR-MARIE FUNCHION 112

Name/Subject Index 133
Scripture Index 135

Preface

by Kaye V. Cook

Professor of Psychology
Gordon College
Wenham, Massachusetts

"The world has gone mad." So proclaims a news article[1] in the wake of the Dallas police shootings in June 2016. Often this madness is attributed to America's love affair with guns, a conclusion that appears to be supported by, for example, the 2012 shootings of twenty children in Sandy Hook, Connecticut. Others bemoan the lack of a moral center in a culture in which religious freedom has become a matter for debate.[2] These analyses may be true, but this "madness" is more globally present, outside the United States as well as within. Some claim that madness (in this case anger more than craziness) led to the passage of Brexit (an abbreviation of "Britain exit"), a June 2016 referendum by which the majority of voters called for the United Kingdom to exit the European Union.[3] Others note that the intense, often irrational anger towards people from other countries that we call xenophobia has sharply increased,[4] perhaps triggered in part by the largest immigration movements in history.[5] The rise of extremist Muslim forces, including

---

1. See, e.g., Pitts, "Our World."
2. Inazu, *Confident Pluralism*.
3. Guida, "Brexit Madness."
4. See news statements during the summer of 2016 for examples. These include statements by Austria's outgoing President Heinz Fischer against xenophobia ("Austria's Outgoing President") and claims of xenophobia as a powerful element in the 2016 United States election (Yan, "Make America White Again").
5. UNHCR, "Global Trends."

Preface

shocking attacks in well-traveled airports (Brussels and Istanbul), is hard to reconcile with a civilized world.

These forms of madness may indeed be the result of a weakened moral center in individuals and institutions—a weakness that allows for mass shootings, sharp class divides, and massive immigration movements to countries without the resources or will to meet basic humanitarian needs. Still, these divisive forces were presumably present in earlier decades and not so strongly felt, perhaps because they were held in check by cultural pressures that have now been modified by modernization.

This book explores pluralism as an agent of cultural change that accompanies modernization and has transformed faith and morality. Some of these transformative influences have been negative, but we propose that others are positive, including potential "formulas for peace,"[6] which make possible coexistence among individuals who ascribe to different faiths and hold different moral standards. In our exploration, we focus particularly on the everyday implications of pluralist theory for Christians and Christian faith.

The broad contours of pluralist theory are easily summarized: pluralism, not secularism, accompanies modernity. Berger's rejection of secularist theory in favor of pluralism seems a boon to Christians. Modernity does not mean that "God is dead"; instead, God is alive and well in modernizing cultures. But in reality, the message is far more complicated. As a result of pluralism, so Berger argues, believers living in cultures that have gone through a modernizing process show the effects of this pluralism in the nature of their faith and churches, as well as in the characteristics of the larger culture in which they live. These changes mean, for example, that faith becomes more uncertain, perhaps empowering fundamentalist movements in an effort to preserve certainty, perhaps leading to a proliferation of cult-like groups that do not maintain the core values of Christianity. The nature of religious institutions also changes so that they become voluntary organizations, forced to compete with children's sports teams and neighborhood social groups for attendees' time and commitment, less able to provide the stability and breadth of community engagement that formerly shaped adolescent and adult identity. Despite these changes, and the shocking examples presented in the opening paragraph, we believe that pluralism has positive results as well as negative—sometimes challenging faith, yet also transforming and strengthening it.

---

6. Hoover, "Pluralist Responses."

Preface

This book began with the happy confluence of Peter Berger's service as Distinguished Visiting Scholar at the Center for Evangelicalism & Culture at Gordon College and the publication of *Many Altars of Modernity*.[7] In this 2014 book, Berger makes a striking and far-reaching observation that the most important effect of modernity on culture is pluralism, not secularism. Many factors illustrate this idea. Globalization increases the flow of people and information across borders, bringing various religions in contact with one another, and modernity gives people greater agency in their personal and political lives. We can observe the effects of these forces at every level of culture, from economic to social, political to personal, and certainly in the arena of religion. Consequently, as Berger points out, every orthodoxy is open to conversation in a new and unfamiliar way.

In his essay for the current volume, Berger resumes this line of thought, acknowledging that while pluralism comes in many forms, such as political pluralism, it is a particular challenge to the orthodoxies of religion. Most religions have a set of shared beliefs about the transcendent—that some things are knowable only by faith—and these beliefs become the basis for living in the world. They serve as the source for community identity and what Berger metaphorically calls the "stranger's address," or the way a person's beliefs locate them in space and time. Not surprisingly for someone whose focus on culture is laser-sharp, Berger has long recognized the problems that pluralism poses for religion. In *Many Altars* most of his examples concern religious pluralism and center around a crucial question: How can religions coexist when each claims to know the truth? This question, which Berger raises anew in his opening chapter, demands further exploration. In this volume, academics in the Christian world address this idea by responding to Berger's opening chapter.

Berger's unique brand of phenomenological sociology is grounded not in the history of ideas, or in economic ideologies, but in the everyday lived experience of human beings. As Berger suggests in his early work with Thomas Luckmann on *The Social Construction of Reality* (1966), knowledge is constructed by the institutions that embody culture and by the individuals who engage it. Religious institutions, far from being lost in modernity, are the primary means by which humans may attempt to manage the uncertainty that is inherent in modernity. People encounter "rumors of angels"[8]—glimpses of transcendence that encourage them to

---

7. Berger, *Many Altars*.
8. Berger, *Rumor of Angels*.

Preface

wager on a spiritual reality. In a pluralist society, knowledge is not enough. When certainty is lost, many individuals recognize their need for God.

Berger proposes that the Schutzian concept of "relevance structures"[9] provides a way to think about religious perspectives and conflicts among them. One's religion originates from transcendent experiences with God and is constructed from these experiences in combination with the "relevances" or abstracted forms of each individual's biographical situation. The resulting constructions may serve as a dynamic framework by which to understand ambiguous events, and are potentially revealed in one's narratives. They may be honed by the beliefs of others, more closely "approximating" or approaching the truth of God in reality (in the language of hermeneutic theory).[10] As Berger notes in the essay that follows, the beliefs that emerge from this process of religious meaning-making may not necessarily map neatly onto the meaning that is institutionalized in faith communities. We may experience *cognitive contamination*, by which our beliefs are influenced by the beliefs of others, both inside and beyond our community. This active process is the result of living in a modernized, globalized world, and may shape our emotions, actions, and cognition.

The stories you will encounter in Berger's essay are illuminating examples of people whose actions enflesh their complicated belief systems: self-flagellating Iranians on the streets of New York, Hare Krishnas dancing in front of a Catholic cathedral in Vienna, and a Chinese man chatting into a cellphone while holding an incense stick in front of an enormous Buddha—perhaps inspiring revulsion, perhaps leading others to question why, or even challenging others to emulate the apparent depth of their commitment. One wonders whether they recognize any incongruity, and in what way such a realization might change their meaning-making processes.

In these stories, Berger describes the real-world implications of the pluralism that modernity engenders. Is it this contextual embeddedness that makes pluralism more descriptive of modernity than secularism? Even sociologists, after all, fall in love, marry, and die. Our humanness inspires us to make meaning, often by craving to be part of something that is larger than ourselves.

Berger's ideas about pluralism have specific implications for Christians. In the essays that follow, authors from within the Christian tradition each speak from a particular stance. They may speak as academics

---

9. Schutz and Luckmann, *Structures of Life-World*.
10. Sandage, Cook, et al., "Hermeneutics and Psychology."

PREFACE

or evangelicals, as political scientists or sociologists, as visitors to places that challenge pluralist theory, or as women who inhabit unique spaces in a complex world—but all speak as Christian believers and academics. Berger himself comments as a committed Lutheran. He builds on Luther's doctrine of two kingdoms, separating the spiritual and the secular, the inner personal life from dimensions that Richard Pierard characterizes as "nature, faith, and politics."[11]

In the ensuing essays, authors take a perspective of thoughtful coexistence with competing beliefs in a global context, while grounded in historic Christian faith. Their essays can be grouped into those that challenge or attempt to nuance Berger's theoretical claims, and those that explore pluralism within a specific cultural context. In the theoretical chapters, the most common challenge is to Berger's belief that there is no such thing as a Christian sociology and that science is value neutral. Sociologist Bruce Wearne discusses how a fully developed Christian scholarly examination of "Faith in a Pluralist Age" should recognize Berger's positive contributions to the discipline and the academy, while at the same time confronting his assumption that there cannot be a Christian sociology. Theologian Roger Olson concurs with Berger that peaceful co-existence is good for everyone, but challenges Berger's ideas about internalized secularity, instead proposing an alternative paradigm of *general providence* for the internal dualism that Berger describes. Political scientist Paul Brink argues that cultures that allow people of various faiths to engage with each other openly—with all their convictional particularities intact—provide a genuinely "public" space in which diverse persons and communities can meet as neighbors and citizens. He contrasts this with the sanitized "secular" space for which some strive in the twenty-first century, and concludes that an appropriate paradigm of pluralism in a religiously complex world must be committed to democracy and human rights, necessarily privileging none but protecting all. Political philosopher James Skillen attempts to replace Berger's description of dualism with a reframing of religion as a way of life, and not simply a way of worship. On this basis, he then demonstrates why support for religious pluralism requires a normative argument for principled pluralism, a particular kind of political system constituted to uphold religious freedom by doing justice to diverse ways of life. These ways of doing justice manifest themselves in the exercise of different kinds of human responsibility in a wide array of social relationships and institutions, as he demonstrates by

---

11. Pierard, "The Lutheran Two-Kingdoms Doctrine."

applying this normative argument to political systems, education, and human responsibility.

In the second section of the book, four authors explore pluralism within the context of culture. This section begins with a chapter by historian Thomas Howard, who argues that the rise of Hindu nationalism in India in recent years, with its communalist ideology, is a striking example of a culture marked by backlashes against pluralism, an example which may suggest modifications to Berger's conclusions or at least raise questions about his paradigm. Philosopher Ruth Groenhout, from a more individualistic feminist perspective, contends that pluralism juxtaposes common Christian arguments about women's anger against feminist perspectives, potentially creating conflict. Her analysis opens possibilities for examining background assumptions about social power and authority that underlie these contrasting pictures of anger, and for thinking about the place of anger in a reasonably healthy life. Ruth Melkonian-Hoover, writing as a political scientist and feminist, draws from interviews with female Brazilian pastors, seminarians, academics, journalists, and politicians to explore whether modern pluralism helps women in Brazil resist patriarchal pressures or further entrenches traditional gendered divisions within families, the church, and the public sphere. Finally, my colleagues and I explore the "stranger's address" by means of two studies. The first describes the values of lay Brazilian and Chinese immigrant Christians, asking whether these retain the markers of their birth country, and the second examines pluralist ideas in the narratives of Brazilian pastors, academics, and thought leaders, and a Chinese pastor/seminary professor. The authors document that even in modernist times values continue to reflect the cultures from which these immigrants come, integrated with the values of their new contexts, revealing their more complicated histories. They further show that pastors, academics, and thought leaders from Brazil and China recognize the challenges of pluralist ideas in the church context, rejecting some competing ideas such as materialism and the prosperity gospel while accepting and integrating others (for example, being willing to embrace social service roles as pastors in response to cultural changes even though feeling called to preach). This "cognitive contamination" is both positive and negative, potentially undermining core Christian beliefs but also and more positively, serving as the basis for the rapid growth of evangelicalism in today's world.

Berger ultimately frames a question that Christians cannot ignore: what are the challenges of pluralism? We have seen pluralist challenges

Preface

played out across the globe, including in the horrific examples that open this chapter, but also "formulas for peace."[12] Berger is right, I believe, when he traces their root cause to pluralism. He suggests that pluralism brings two challenges: the problem of secular spaces, and that of pluralism's relativizing influence. None of these essays accepts Berger's dualistic resolution of the problem of secular spaces, addressed specifically by each of the first four papers, but several explore pluralism's relativizing influence, most notably the last chapter by Cook, Chang, and Funchion. Berger also highlights three benefits of pluralism, suggesting that pluralism clarifies the nature of faith as trust in God rather than certainty about what one believes, shifts churches toward being voluntary and away from being obligatory associations in which one has membership by birth, and requires differentiating the non-negotiable core of faith from more peripheral beliefs that one is willing to let go. Several essays illustrate the first two promises, most directly the chapter by Melkonian-Hoover, and several refine or challenge the third promise, as do the chapters by Brink and Skillen. The last chapter concludes by saying that pluralism, with all its challenges, opens up new possibilities for understanding one's own faith and for changing culture, agreeing with Berger's conclusion in his opening chapter: Pluralism, though challenging, is good for Christian faith.

Each participant in this book attempts to explore fundamental questions raised by Berger's pluralist theory using the methods of his or her discipline and from the perspective of faith. We thus provide theological and personal reflections on Berger's ideas, as he himself requests. This is a sociological challenge worthy of careful attention, but even more broadly it is a moral, cultural, and religious challenge. We offer this collection of essays in an effort to begin the conversation that these challenges deserve.

Sadly, Peter Berger died before the manuscript reached publication. I am grateful for his unique, creative, perceptive insights on the nature of faith in modernizing times. I regret that he will not have a chance to respond to the excellent comments—most supportive, some challenging—in response to this opening chapter, his last publication. Peter often quoted Julian of Norwich to me. I quote her now: Turn the earth upside down, and seek the deepness.[13] You did indeed, Peter. Thank you.

---

12. Hoover, "Pluralist Responses."
13. Doyle, "Meditations," 84.

Preface

Bibliography

"Austria's Outgoing President Warns Against Populism and Xenophobia." *Euronews* (July 8, 2016). http://www.euronews.com/2016/07/08/austria-s-outgoing-president-warns-against-populism-and-xenophobia.

Berger, Peter. *A Rumor of Angels: Modern Society and the Rediscovery of the Supernatural.* Garden City, NY: Doubleday, 1969.

Berger, Peter. *The Many Altars of Modernity: Toward a Paradigm for Religion in a Pluralist Age.* Berlin: De Gruyter Mouton, 2014.

Berger, Peter, and Thomas Luckmann. *The Social Construction of Reality: A Treatise in the Sociology of Knowledge.* Garden City, NY: Anchor/Doubleday, 1966.

Doyle, Brendan, ed. *Meditations with Julian of Norwich.* Santa Fe, NM: Bear, 1983.

Guida, Victoria. "Brexit Madness." (June 2016). http://www.politico.com/tipsheets/morning-trade/2016/06/brexit-madness-215005.

Hoover, Dennis R. "Pluralist Responses to Pluralist Realities in the United States." *Society* 53 (2016) 20–27.

Inazu, John D. *Confident Pluralism: Surviving and Thriving Through Deep Difference.* Chicago, IL: University of Chicago Press, 2016.

Pierard, Richard V. "The Lutheran Two-Kingdoms Doctrine and Subservience to the State in Modern Germany." *JETS* 29.2 (1986) 193–203.

Pitts, Leonard. "Our World Has Gone Mad." *Salisbury Post* (July 8, 2016). http://www.salisburypost.com/2016/07/08/leonard-pitts-our-world-has-gone-mad/.

Sandage, Steven J., Kaye V. Cook, Peter C. Hill, Brad D. Strawn, and Kevin S. Reimer, "Hermeneutics and Psychology: A Review and Dialectical Model." *Review of General Psychology* 12 (2008) 344–64.

Schutz, Alfred, and Luckmann, Thomas. *The Structures of the Life-World.* Translated by Richard M. Zanere and H. Tristram Engelhardt. Evanston, IL: Northwestern University Press, 1973.

United Nations High Commissioner for Refugees (UNHCR). "Global Trends: Forced Displacement in 2015." http://www.unhcr.org/statistics/unhcrstats/576408cd7/unhcr-global-trends-2015.html?query=global-trends-2015.

Yan, Holly. "'Make America White Again': Hate Speech and Crimes Post-Election." (November 29, 2016). http://www.cnn.com/2016/11/10/us/post-election-hate-crimes-and-fears-trnd.

Acknowledgement

This project was made possible through the support of a grant from the John Templeton Foundation. The opinions expressed in this publication are those of the author(s) and do not necessarily reflect the views of the John Templeton Foundation.

1

Faith in a Pluralist Age

by Peter L. Berger

Professor Emeritus of Religion, Sociology and Theology,
Boston University (2009–2017).
Founder and former Director of the Institute on Culture,
Religion, and World Affairs (CURA) at Boston University.
Author, *The Many Altars of Modernity: Toward a Paradigm for
Religion in a Pluralist Age* (2014).

Prelude

This paper proposes that the most important effect of modernity on religion is not—as still widely assumed—secularization, but pluralism. It is not, as Nietzsche believed, that God is dead, but that there are too many gods. This must be seen in the context of globalization. Everyone communicates with everyone else—literally by physically hopping around all over the planet—migrants, tourists, business people, military people, terrorists (they communicate by bombs). Religion is not immune to this global chatter. We learn in Social Psychology 101 that people who keep talking with each other influence each other. That is why the Apostle Paul urged Christians not to be "yoked together with unbelievers." Unbelief and doubt can be infectious. So can faith. I call this very important process (which can go either way) cognitive contamination. It is a threat to every orthodoxy. Only psychopaths are truly immune to it. (Incidentally, there are practitioners of religions that emphasize right practice over right belief, such as some Jews and Hindus, who claim that their ortho*praxis* avoids the pitfalls of orthodox Christian dogma. That is not convincing, if only because every new generation of children will ask questions. The child of observant Jews will ask, "Just *why* was I not allowed to eat those delicious ham sandwiches?" The child of Brahmins will ask, "Why did you refuse to hire this nice fellow as a cook because you found out that his caste was too low?" The answers to such questions are doxy/dogma.)

I read somewhere that travelers meeting in ancient Greece would ask, "Which are your gods?" This was asking the stranger's address, as we would ask for someone's area code or postal code. If one knew a person's address, one knew his or her religion. It was so in Germany until after World War II. When the Peace of Westphalia ended the Thirty Years' War, its most important decision was that the ruler would decide whether his state would be Catholic or Protestant; those who didn't like the decision were allowed to emigrate (certainly an improvement over being killed or forcibly converted). Of course, there have been some population movements in Germany since then, but until quite recently if you knew that someone was from the Rhineland you could assume that he was Catholic; if from Saxony, Protestant. This is no longer so, because of the enormous demographic shifts since the war. Also, because there are no more state churches, individual German citizens can change church affiliation or have no affiliation at all.

The Austrian sociologist of religion Paul Zulehner has titled his recent book about religious changes in his country *Verbuntung* ("making more colorful"). Religious changes in Austria have indeed made Austria more colorful, as is also true of western and central Europe, and much of the world. Some years ago I had lunch in Vienna, my hometown, in a restaurant overlooking the square in front of St. Stephen's, one of the great cathedrals of medieval Christendom. Some strange noises were coming up from the square. It turned out to be a group of Hare Krishna devotees chanting and dancing; they all appeared to be white Austrians. There was a traffic jam some time ago on Park Avenue in New York: the street was jammed by a procession of Iranians celebrating the Shia festival of Ashura, in which penance is performed to commemorate the Holy Martyrs. There were several hundred men marching to the beat of drums. They were all stripped to the waist; they whipped themselves until blood poured down their backs. Iran has not been very popular in the U.S. for quite a while; some pedestrians watched the spectacle with very little sympathy. Scores of NYPD officers were marching along on either side of the parade, their faces expressionless—New York cops have seen *everything*. During the Christmas season the Ginza, Tokyo's main shopping area, is full of Christmas ornaments and the PA system blares out the customary American carols. (Perhaps this should not be mentioned in the context of religious globalization; if the Japanese shoppers were worshipping at anything, it was at the shrine of capitalist consumerism.) But I should mention one other incident: On a walk in Hong Kong I passed a Buddhist temple and stepped inside. A Chinese man was standing in front of a huge statue of the Buddha, slightly bowed. In his right hand he was holding a burning incense stick; in his left hand he held a mobile phone into which he has talking (to whom or what, I wondered for a moment).

Cultural globalization is often perceived as a process of Westernization or, even more specifically, Americanization. There is some merit to this perception. The dissemination of Western ideas, values, and behaviors is very powerful. In the matter of religion, the immense explosion of Pentecostalism in the Global South may be seen as a form of Americanization, despite the successful indigenization of the movement wherever it has taken hold; it still shows the traces of its origins in Los Angeles a little over a century ago. But Tulasi Srinivas, an Indian anthropologist, uses the concept of "counter-emissions" in describing the influences going in the other direction: Many Americans practice yoga and other forms of Asian meditation, and believe in reincarnation; U.S. medical schools are interested in Indian and Chinese methods of healing; the Vedanta Society has a center on the campus of Boston University; there are an estimated 800,000 American converts to Buddhism (with some sixty centers just in the Greater Boston area).

The Apostle was right on this: Sustained conversation with unbelievers threatens alleged religious certainties. Fundamentalism is the project to prevent such conversation.

Many observers of the contemporary world still think that we live in a secular age. The assumption is that modernity necessarily pushes religion toward the margins of society and of the consciousness of individuals. Some who think this and welcome this perceived state of affairs are in the tradition of the Enlightenment, which celebrated the victory of reason over religious superstition. I suppose a ceremonial climax of this celebration was when the French revolutionaries crowned a streetwalker as the goddess of reason in the solemnly desacralized Church of the Madeleine in Paris. Others agree with the assumption, but deplore rather than welcome it. Thus

Pope Francis calls for a new evangelism, to reconvert to the faith what has become a godless world (especially, but not only, in Europe).

The assumption that we are in a secular age came to be known as "secularization theory"; there were some good arguments for it, and it dominated the study of contemporary religion by the middle of the twentieth century, when I started my career as a sociologist. It took me some twenty years to come to the conclusion that the empirical evidence does not support the theory. Most of the world today is as religious as it ever was, and in some places, more so. I would like to emphasize that this change of mind on my part was not caused by some kind of religious conversion: My religious position, a theologically open-minded Lutheranism, has not changed during my adult life. What changed was my reading of the empirical evidence.

An obvious question arises: If secularization theory must be given up, what could take its place? Over a period of years, it occurred to me that what should replace it is a theory of pluralism. We don't live in a secular age. We live in a pluralist age. This greatly affects the place of religion in society and in the lives of individuals. It constitutes a challenge for faith, but it is different from the assumed challenge of secularity. In 2014 I published a book that made a first stab at a new theory: *The Many Altars of Modernity: Toward a Paradigm for Religion in a Pluralist Age*. Writing it was an exercise in sociological analysis, without any religious presupposition. (There cannot be Christian sociology, any more than Christian chemistry or Christian automotive engineering.) I could have written the same book as a Buddhist, an atheist, or whatever. However, it so happens that I am a Christian believer, concerned with the implications of my findings for my faith. So this essay is a theological reflection about my sociological findings. It can be summed up as a suggestion to my fellow believers: *Do not be afraid of pluralism. It is good for you!*

I propose that our age is actually marked by two pluralisms. There is religious pluralism as commonly understood: several religions co-existing, more or less peacefully, in the same society. Then there is the co-existence between religious discourses and a powerful secular discourse, originally rooted in modern science and technology. Its power comes from the enormously successful way in which scientifically based technology has changed the human condition, mostly for the better. (Critics of modernity should reflect on the fact that in pre-modern societies most children died before the age of five; today, even in poor countries, most children live into adulthood.) Secularization theory was not completely wrong, in that it recognized the importance of the secular discourse; it just greatly exaggerated its capacity to push out religious discourses.

Religion and secularity are often seen as being essentially antagonistic. That may be true of a very small portion of people, those totally committed to either faith or its denial. For most religious people it is not a matter of either/or but rather of both/and. (An important distinction should be made here between *secularity* and *secularism*. The latter term, as the suffix suggests, is a view that rejects religion as a whole, which may range from militant atheism to a less violent disdain for an alleged illusion—or that wants religion kept out of the public arena, for the sake of civic peace. In other words, secularism is a philosophical worldview or a political ideology. The term *secularity*, on the other hand, describes the fact that there are areas of life that are handled without reference to religion—such as sociology.)

There probably has always been a distinction between sacred and profane activities. Modernity has led to a great expansion of the space allowed for secularity, and not only due to the role of science and technology. Hugo Grotius (1583–1646), the Dutch jurist who was one of the founders of modern international law, proposed that this new discipline should be developed "as if God did not exist" (*etsi Deus non daretur*)—that is, without any religious presuppositions. He hardly had a choice: Europe in his time was divided between states defined as Catholic or Protestant and different varieties of Protestantism, as well as Eastern Orthodox Russia and the Muslim Ottoman Empire, so a law intended to cover all of these had to be free of any particular religious presuppositions. (It should be noted that if Grotius' formula is to be called "atheist," it is as a methodological atheism rather than a philosophical one. Grotius was a pious Protestant, belonging to the Arminian denomination, which I would call the more humane branch of the Dutch Reformation. The strict Calvinists who were then in power in the newly independent Netherlands forced Grotius into exile in relatively more tolerant Germany.) One can see here very clearly how pluralism on an international scale opened up a space for secular discourse; the same happened in the Netherlands domestically a little later (Grotius could have stayed at home then). In any case, pluralism does not necessarily secularize, but for very practical reasons pluralism creates social spaces for secular (religiously neutral) institutions. Needless to say, religious institutions (the churches in Christian Europe) had to find ways to accept these secular spaces, even if they had theological qualms—unless they were to engage in ongoing religious warfare.

One of the theological questions pluralism raises for the churches and for individuals is how to accept the secular spaces. Different Christian churches have different ways of doing this. The Roman Catholic Church can use its long tradition of natural law, which is supposedly relevant both to the revealed truth in the custody of the Church and to the universal moral principles inscribed in all human hearts. The Reformed tradition's all-encompassing notion of a Christian commonwealth—for example, in New England and in South Africa—makes it more difficult to accept secular spaces. However, one of the most interesting modern Reformed theologians, Abraham Kuyper, made a vigorous stab at it with his idea of "sphere sovereignty"—that not every area of social life must be directly governed in every detail by the ultimate sovereignty of Christ. In addition to being a very conservative Calvinist theologian, Kuyper was also a practical politician who served as prime minister of the Netherlands from 1901 to 1905. He devised the system of "pillars"—by which every denomination and worldview was allocated its own zone of publicly supported influence. (On my first visit to the Netherlands, many years ago, I went for a walk and came across an office with a sign on the door, "Protestant Electricians Union.") Lutherans have developed their own theological rationale for accepting secular spaces by their sharp distinction between Law and Gospel (doctrine of the "Two Realms")—succinctly expressed by Luther in his saying "I'd rather be ruled by a just Turk than by an unjust Christian."

There are different theological ideas capable of inspiring "formulas of peace" between different religions and value systems in pluralistic situations—from the "*conviviencia*" of Muslims, Christians and Jews during the better years of Muslim rule in Spain—to the separation of religion and the state in the First Amendment to the U.S. Constitution (which of course presupposes a secular space in the law). Let me just add an important corollary: If secular spaces are to be allowed in society, they must also be allowed in individual consciousness. Put differently, if the First Amendment is to function in American society, there must be its miniaturized version in the minds of citizens.

How is this possible? All religions, from the most primitive to the most sophisticated, deal with the ultimate concerns of the human condition. Certainly Christian faith does. However, many penultimate concerns must be addressed in the business of living. I think that the social theory of Alfred Schutz (1900–1959) has produced some useful concepts to analyze how different ultimate and penultimate "multiple realities" co-exist in the mind (although Schutz himself was quite uninterested in religion). This is even the case with individuals who believe they have direct contact with divine or supernatural realities. In such experiences the reality of everyday life, what Schutz called the "paramount reality," fades away, and the individual enters a truly different world. (Schutz characterized it as a "finite province of meaning.") Take one of the great Catholic mystics, Teresa of Avila (1515–1582), whose encounters with God certainly tore her out of ordinary reality. However, Teresa (along with her friend San Juan de la Cruz) was very active reforming the Carmelite order in Spain, and in pursuit of this task I assume that she periodically examined the financial accounts of convents under her direction. It is very difficult to do arithmetic while in the throes of spiritual ecstasy, and vice versa.

For most ordinary believers, the Schutzian concept of "relevance structures" is more applicable. Religious actions and ideas co-exist with secular ones, without necessarily colliding. As far as I know, Pope Francis I is not a mystic, so perhaps he can switch religious and secular relevances more easily than Teresa. Imagine him on an errand with an explicitly religious relevance—say, going to a ceremony where he will promulgate someone's status as a new saint. He is to be driven in the famous white "popemobile" (which looks rather like an outsized golf cart). The popemobile won't start. What will his aides do? I think they will call a garage mechanic, not an exorcist.

The capacity of human beings to switch relevances has presumably been there from the beginnings of the species. Modern people have to develop this capacity to a very high degree, because social life has become very complex; there are lots of relevance structures to navigate through, even in a single day. Pluralism vastly increases the multiplicity of relevance structures. Religion is no exception to this development.

There are good reasons why religious believers in any tradition should be disturbed by the challenge of pluralism. But Christians might usefully reflect about the curious resemblance between our contemporary situation and that of the early church. Palestine in the days of Jesus was hardly a religiously monolithic place; Galilee, in particular, was a religiously diverse region, with Jews and Gentiles interspersed and presumably interacting. By the time the Apostle Paul started out on his missionary journeys, the late Roman Empire was one of the most pluralistic civilizations in history. If one wants a snapshot of this pluralism there is no better text than the account of Paul's sermon in Athens in which he noted the many objects of worship he saw in the city, including the altar dedicated to an "unknown god," whom he then proceeded to identify with the God who created the world and who raised Jesus from the dead. The Athenians were apparently intrigued by this message, and at least two were convinced. They and all the other converts who followed had to *choose* to follow this Jesus. Christian faith was totally new; there was no alternative of falling back to a taken-for-granted Christian tradition—there was no such tradition! Kierkegaard, who attacked the relaxed traditionalism of the Danish state church of his day and called for a faith based on a passionate "leap" into the unknown, suggested that Christians should "become contemporaneous with Jesus." That, I think, would require quite an effort. But it is remarkably easy to put ourselves into the pluralistic situation of the early Christians (at least in the big cities of the Mediterranean world). We are already in that situation! I don't think that this is something to bemoan.

Religious conservatives argue that pluralism relativizes the affirmations of faith. There is no denying that they have a point. If I believe that X is true, the very presence of an individual who firmly believes in Y relativizes my belief, to the extent that it no longer seems self-evident. But pluralism means that I am surrounded not just by many Ys, but also by As, Bs, and Zs. Even minimal reflectiveness at any level of sophistication, by ditch diggers as well as philosophers, means that I must choose between these options (on whatever level of sophistication, by philosophers as well as ditch diggers). Modernization can generally be described as a movement from fate to choice—from choosing which tools to use, to choosing which gods to worship. This is but another way of saying that pluralism increases the zone of freedom. I suppose that it is a philosophical question whether this is a good or a bad thing: It is good if one values freedom, bad if one values a tranquil, undisturbed mind. The Spanish thinker Miguel de Unamuno (1814–1936) is best known for his book *The Tragic Sense of Life*, which I understand as a hymn to Don Quixote as an icon of freedom. It ends with a wish for the reader: "May God give you not peace but glory."

Is religion as fate preferable to religion as free choice? Yes, if religion is a congenital condition, like a particular hair color or allergy. Freedom inevitably creates anxiety. This elementary fact is nicely illustrated by a classic American joke—a conversation between two friends: "Have you found a job?"—"Yes, but it's a terrible job."—"Just what do you do?"—"I sit in the shade under a tree in an orange grove. I have three baskets in front of me. I put the big oranges in the first basket, the little oranges in the second basket, the in-between oranges in the third. And that's what I do all day long."—"I don't get it. Sounds to me like a rather comfortable job. What's so terrible about it?"—"*All those decisions!*"

Freedom can be a burden. Erich Fromm (1900–1980), in his classical study of the psychology of totalitarianism, gave it the title *Escape from Freedom*. If freedom is a burden, then escape is fundamentalism. It can be religious or secular, and indeed can have any cognitive or behavioral content. It is based on allegedly certain beliefs and it bestows an allegedly certain identity. It is fierce in repelling or repressing any criticisms. It is almost impossible to reason with it.

A Theological Defense of Pluralism

I have given an overview of the pluralistic context in which faith finds itself today. I propose that there are three theological benefits from this context: a new insight into the nature of faith; a new insight into the nature of the church; and a way of distinguishing the core of the faith from its more peripheral aspects.

A New Insight into the Nature of Faith in the Context of Pluralism

The Apostle Paul (in Romans 3:28) told of "being justified by faith without the works of the law." This was deliberately amplified by Luther, who sneaked the word *alone* into his translation of the phrase—"by faith *alone*." This was not due to Luther's bad Greek as a translator, nor to a deliberate deception. Rather, he thought that the amplification was in accord with Paul's basic intention, which was to free the new Christian faith from obedience to the Jewish law. That was not Luther's problem in the sixteenth century, but he now put this in a new context, that of freeing the faith from what he regarded as the legalism ("works righteousness") of the Roman Church. "*Sola fide*" became the battle cry of the Protestant Reformation against Rome. But I don't think that today we have to be stuck with a polemical understanding of either Jewish or Roman "works righteousness." Our contemporary pluralistic context provides new insight into the meaning of *sola fide*. The phrase can now be understood as an acceptance of the loss of certainty that results from the relativizing effect of pluralism. Another way of putting this: The phrase denotes acceptance of the penumbra of doubt that goes with faith that no longer is taken for granted.

Faith in a Pluralist Age

It is very common for preachers in different Christian denominations to counterpose faith and unbelief, and to represent the latter as rebellion against God, or at least as a grave sin. I think that this counter-position is misleading: The opposite of faith is not unbelief; it is knowledge. As I write this I look from the window of my study at the skyline of Boston; I know that I am in Boston, not in New York, or London, or any other locality. I don't need faith to conclude that I am in Boston. To be sure, a beginning graduate student could argue with me—maybe I'm dreaming this, maybe my vision is disturbed by an eye disease—can I really *prove* that what I see from my window is real? the graduate student asks . . . . He can question as much as he wants, but I still know what I see; he and I are just playing a game here. There is the classic story of the eighteenth-century conversation between the philosopher Bishop George Berkeley and the famous *litterateur* Dr. Samuel Johnson. They were out on a walk, and Bishop Berkeley was trying to convince Dr. Johnson that there was no way to prove that the outside world is real and not just in the mind. Dr. Johnson listened with increasing irritation, then kicked a stone across the road and said, "Thus I disprove you!"

Schutz would say that the session in my study is squarely in the "paramount reality" of everyday life, which is so powerful that only a sort of mystical experience could pull me out of it. But suppose now that I am out on a walk with my friend Jack, whom I have known for many years and who has always acted toward me very affectionately. I have just read about yet another case of a man who, without a rational motive, pulled out a gun and killed a bunch of bystanders. The people who knew this person often say, when interviewed after the event, that he was the nicest guy, always friendly, seemingly normal. Then I find myself thinking, "Do I really know that Jack is not a psychopathic murderer, who will pull out a gun any moment and shoot me?" I will probably tell myself that of course I cannot *know* this, but I know enough about him so as to have *faith* in his benevolence.

This reflection is very relevant to an understanding of Christian faith. *Sola fide* means that I cannot *know* the truth of the Gospel; I have *faith* in it. Christianity is not a secret knowledge (*gnosis*) into which one can be initiated (as was done in the many mystery cults and gnostic schools that competed with Christianity in its early days). It was, and still is, an act of faith in the truth of the Gospel. As the author of the Letter to the Hebrews put it, "Faith is the assurance of things hoped for, the conviction of things not seen" (Hebrews 11:1, RSV). Luther made a Latin word play to make this point: Faith/*fides* is trust/*fiducia*—trust in the goodness of God disclosed by Jesus Christ. Luther once remarked: "I don't really know *what* I believe, I know *in whom* I believe." (I'm not suggesting Luther hero worship. There are some very unsavory aspects to the man, especially in his later years— such as the vicious anti-Semitism of his tract *Against the Jews and their Lies*, and his endorsement of the bloody suppression of the Peasant Rebellion. But at the end of the day, I find the Lutheran understanding of Christianity more persuasive than many others.)

Coming to Terms with Churches as Voluntary Associations

Almost all Christian churches have in the past made aggressive, if not exclusive, claims regarding the truth of their particular version of Christianity. Very often the same churches had been established by the state in the past, and now find it difficult to do without this kind of support. No longer can one rely on the state to fill one's pews; lay people have to be persuaded to sit in the pews and, once sitting there, to keep on doing so. This changes the relationship between clergy and laity; inevitably, the latter become more powerful. It also changes the relationship between churches, from potential opponents in religious conflict to competitors in what, if pluralism is combined with religious freedom, is in effect a religious market. Rodney Stark and other sociologists identified with the "supply-side school" in the study of religion have seen competition as the main factor making for religious vitality. This is very likely an exaggeration. The democratic societies of Western Europe have religious freedom as much as the United States and are moving toward ever more pluralism. Yet Europe is still much more secularized than the U.S. The historian Richard Niebuhr argued in his classic work *The Social Sources of Denominationalism* (1929) that America has created a new kind of religious institution—the "denomination." European sociologists of religion (notably Max Weber and Ernst Troeltsch) distinguished between two types of religious institutions, the "church" and the "sect"—the former a large body into which one is born, the latter a small tightly-knit group which one *joins*. Niebuhr proposed that the denomination is an institution that combines the characteristics of the aforementioned types: a large body, not necessarily tightly-knit, which one has decided to join and in which one decides to stay. Of course, Niebuhr's new type has a distinctly American flavor (as, by the way, has Rodney Stark's approach). However, without any direct American influence, the combination of religious pluralism and religious freedom produces a "denominationalizing" effect in many countries (even in Europe, where a few years ago there was a Pentecostal congress in Dublin with some ten thousand attendees!).

The most dramatic case of a religious institution accepting its new social reality as a voluntary association, albeit very reluctantly, is that of the Roman Catholic Church between the First and the Second Vatican Council, within the span of one century between the 1860s and 1960s. Vatican I was convened by Pope Pius IX, author of the Index of Prohibited Books, which condemned the basic features of modernity, proclaimed the doctrine of papal infallibility, and insisted on the freedom of the Church to proclaim the truth entrusted to it (but with the proviso that error has no rights). Vatican II, convened by the open-minded Pope John XXIII, radically changed the tone with which the world was addressed, called for dialogue with all other religions and with those with no religion, and (most importantly) declared religious freedom to be a basic right of all human beings, not just Catholics. Without conceding that some of its doctrines may need to be revised, the Church willy-nilly accepted the fact that, empirically speaking, it had become a voluntary association/denomination. Not accidentally, two of the most important consultants of the Council were from two Western home countries of democracy: John Courtney Murray of the U.S. and Jacques Maritain of France.

Religious freedom protects religious pluralism. But pluralism also provides the political rationale (if not the necessity) for religious freedom. Specifically, the secular, religiously neutral space that pluralism opens up can be used as the most practical setting for the political management of pluralism (which is generally less costly than repression).

The Core and the Periphery

Finally, the relativization of taken-for-granted religion, which pluralism brings about, leads to a process I call "cognitive bargaining." As I converse with "the others," they who do not share my worldview, we influence each other. Only rarely does this lead to conversion in either direction; I don't surrender my worldview to theirs, and they don't surrender to mine (though of course this does happen). More commonly there is a give-and-take: I'll let you have X, but I'll stick to Y. This has what I think is a very positive outcome. I am forced to distinguish the non-negotiable core of my faith from more peripheral features that I'm prepared to let go.

There is a wonderful story about the great Hillel the Elder (110 BCE–10 CE), one of the founders of rabbinical Judaism. He was once asked (in mockery, I suspect) whether he could explain the meaning of Torah while standing on one foot. He said yes, and then recited the first recorded formulation of the Golden Rule—"Don't do to others what you hate being done to you." (Christians generally think that, as reported in the New Testament, this sentence was invented by Jesus. More likely, Jesus was quoting Hillel). With all due respect to this great teacher, I think that Hillel made a poor choice. The sentence only refers to the Second Tablet of the Law, the one that deals with relations with other people rather than the relation with God. It seems to me that he would have been better advised to recite the Shema, the one sentence proclaiming the faith of Israel, which has been on the lips of so many pious Jews as they faced death: "Hear O Israel, the Lord is our God, the Lord is one." Be this as it may, after reciting the sentence while standing on one foot, Hillel added a profound afterword: *"The rest is commentary."* Muslims (possibly describable as the spiritual great-grandchildren of Hillel) would have no difficulty in coming up with the one core sentence explaining their faith, the Shehada: "There is no God but Allah, and Muhammad is his messenger."

What about Christianity?

I think the core message of the Gospel concerns the resurrection of Jesus Christ. It is the one miracle that (however interpreted) is nonnegotiable. To say this, of course, raises a lot of questions. Was there an empty tomb after Jesus rose from the dead?—put differently, if a police camera had been installed in the tomb, what would it have shown as the body of Jesus disappeared? What was the nature of the body of the risen Christ, which in the New Testament accounts is clearly different from a revived corpse? And what is the consequence of the resurrection of Christ for the future of all humans, and indeed for the future of the entire unredeemed cosmos—caught majestically in the words of the Orthodox Easter liturgy as the risen Christ "trampled death with death"? Once again I take my cue from the Apostle Paul: "If Christ be not risen, then is our preaching vain, and your faith is also vain" (1 Corinthians 15:14). The Christian Shema: "'Christ is risen'—the rest is commentary." But what about all the other miracles recounted in the New Testament? For example, did Jesus walk on the water in the Sea of Galilee? If he was who he said he was, I cannot exclude this possibility. But neither am I constrained to affirm it. My faith is certainly not "vain" without it.

I will conclude with a story from the (happily defunct) Soviet Union. Periodically the Communist Party conducted campaigns to promote "scientific atheism." During one such campaign all the inhabitants of a village, including the Orthodox priest, had to assemble for a one-hour lecture by a Party official about the truth of atheism and the illusions of religion. When he was finished, the official said: "We believe in free speech here (the hell they did!)—the priest will have five minutes for rebuttal." The priest came up front and said, "I don't need five minutes." Then he turned to the assembled villagers and said: "Christ is risen!" The villagers responded with the proper liturgical sequel: "He is risen indeed!" The priest then returned to where he had stood among the congregation.

Postlude

As mentioned earlier, religious pluralism was brought to public attention in America by the World Parliament of Religion in 1893. Publicity was ensured by making this conference part of the Chicago World's Fair, which was a big tourist attraction. Mixed in with industrial and agricultural exhibits from many countries there was religion, the more exotic the better. Swami Vivekananda introduced Hinduism with a speech addressed to "brothers and sisters of America." (The sisters were particularly impressed.) The speech focused on the Ramakrishna (1836–1886), an important figure of the Hindu revival that flourished in Bengal in the nineteenth century, who argued that all religions are essentially the same. An itinerant religious entrepreneur from Lebanon gave a series of lectures about the Baha'i faith. Abdul-Baha, the son of the Prophet Baha'Ullah, had fled with his father from Iran to the Ottoman Empire, and was now living in a village in Palestine. The first lecture began with the announcement that Jesus had returned to earth and was living in the Holy Land. Several American "sisters" subsequently traveled to the village of Bahji, near Haifa. Abdul-Baha made two missionary journeys to America; the Baha'i headquarters in the U.S. is still in a suburb of Chicago, the world headquarters in Haifa.

The rather dramatic arrival of Asian religion in America stimulated a flurry of interest in interreligious dialogue between Christianity and the traditions originating in the Indian subcontinent, especially Hinduism and Buddhism. The beginnings of the ecumenical movement in the early twentieth century stimulated a flurry of intra-Christian dialogue. Since its founding in 1948, the World Council of Churches has pursued this type of dialogue, much of it at its headquarters in Geneva. The Second Vatican Council, which ended in 1965, led to the creation of an entire dialogue machinery in the Vatican itself. A number of centers were established. One was devoted to dialogue with so-called "separated brethren," meaning non-Catholic Christians; this rather patronizing term has since been dropped. One was focused on conducting dialogue with Jews, whose very special relation with Christians was solemnly affirmed by the Council; understandably, much of it has been concerned with the Christian roots of anti-Semitism and with the religious status, if any, of the State of Israel. Then there was founded an agency concerned with dialogue with other religions. What happened was rather funny: Someone noticed that this left out a rather big chunk of humanity—those who had no religion at all. Surely an organization calling itself universal should enter into dialogue with them, too! Cardinal Koenig, the Archbishop of Vienna, was put in charge of that operation, the Secretariat for Non-Believers. The question was how to find them! You could hardly have dialogue with people that were unorganized. Thus in 1969 the Cardinal convoked a conference in Rome with the warrant to find the non-believers and to develop ideas of how to talk with them. The second question was basically theological, the first sociological. I was still absurdly young then, but I had written a few things that someone had read, so I was asked to bring together a group of social scientists, of any faith or none, who had dealt with religion in the contemporary world. We spent a fascinating working week in Rome. (Somewhere I may still have some letters on stationery of the Secreteratius Pro Non-Credentibus). Since then a veritable cottage industry of religious dialogue has developed all over the place, not only in Geneva and Rome. Pluralism has indeed developed some odd offspring!

I have continued to be interested in interreligious dialogue, both because it is intellectually interesting and because it can be useful in the cause of peace. (Since 9/11 there has been much conversation with Muslims in the U.S.) However, one must keep in mind that in a pluralistic situation, such dialogue occurs on two levels. There is dialogue between intellectuals, typically in conference centers or seminar rooms; there is also conversation between ordinary people with very different levels of education who want to understand each other, which may take place in homes or around the water fountain at workplaces. It is important to understand the difference.

In the 1970s the World Council of Churches convoked a study group consisting of theologians from most Christian denominations, including the Orthodox, with the warrant to re-examine the *filioque*. This was an important issue leading to the historic schism in the eleventh century between the Eastern/Greek and Western/Latin branches of Christianity. The Latin word was inserted by the Roman Catholic Church into the Nicene Creed, which in its third article affirms faith in "the Holy Spirit who proceeds from the Father, and with the Father and Son is worshipped and glorified." The *filioque* "and from the Son" was inserted after the first mention of "the Father." The reason for this, as far as I know, was that the Arian heresy which had been condemned by the Council of Nicea (convoked in CE 325 by the Emperor Constantine, whose motives were primarily political rather than theological) had survived and was popping up again six centuries later in the West. The idea behind the insertion was to strengthen the doctrine of the Trinity. The East saw it differently: For complicated reasons the Orthodox thought that the *filioque* actually weakened the doctrine of the Trinity. More importantly, they thought that the Latin Church did not have the right to alter unilaterally the wording of a creed agreed upon by the first ecumenical council. Constantinople and Rome ended up excommunicating each other, and they remain formally not in full communion with each other. I think it is reasonable to assume that the political rivalry for primacy between these two centers had at least as much to do with the split as disagreements over the inner workings of the Trinity. Without in any way disparaging the usefulness of the WCC project on the *filioque*, which I read at the time with considerable interest, one must observe that the laity of both ecclesial communities had no interest in this dispute. Indeed, most of them had probably never heard of it. Thus, when in liturgical churches any of the great creeds is recited to solemnly affirm what "we believe," what is really going on is an affirmation of what "we *are supposed to* believe." That is true of all variants of interfaith or intra-faith dialogue. That is why many of these dialogue exercises make one think of border negotiations between nonexistent countries.

Pluralism has benefits for faith. The reflection toward which it pushes believers is also beneficial, on every level of sophistication, because it deepens the question of what I myself—and not just some abstract community to which I am supposed to belong—*really* believe.

2

Christian Sociology between Appreciation, Dissent, Communication, and Contribution

Bruce C. Wearne

Senior Lecturer (retired), Monash University
Port Lonsdale, Australia

Introduction

The first words I ever read of Peter Berger's work are in the preface to his 1963 *Invitation to Sociology*: "This book is intended to be read, not studied."[1] I wonder: should this guide me now in response to Berger's opening chapter? Of course, in critical evaluation of a theorist's work one must respect authorial intent. But therein lies the problem with interpreting Berger's wide-ranging contributions to sociology. As was true of Berger's earlier *Invitation*, "Faith in a Pluralist Age" beckons us beyond mere reading and toward a more careful inquiry into the implied theoretical system that Berger has artfully and provocatively presented. Berger's intensely reflective essay contains in a nutshell the outline of an entire sociological research program. As such it is another wide-angled, "vintage Berger" contribution. But my effort here is limited to an autobiographical exploration of Berger's bracketed statement in "Faith in a Pluralist Age" about the impossibility of Christian sociology and then some brief comments about his contributions to the academic field of sociology.

In the paragraphs that follow, I will use my own experience to explain why I dissent from Berger's provocative statement. My defense of the validity of a Christian sociology arises from a philosophical conviction that any

---

1. Berger, *Invitation*, 7.

sociology in its theorizing cannot avoid its dependence upon pre-scientific assumptions of a religious character. Peter Berger has indeed made a salient contribution to sociology, but can his insistence upon a strict duality in the life of the Christian student, scholar, or scientist be viewed as a necessary precondition for sociology? Berger's stringent denial seems designed to allay Christian misunderstanding, a concern that indicates a pastoral sensitivity which has always characterized his work. He believes that Christians, and Christian students in particular, will benefit from wise, scientifically-honed advice that *inter alia* points them away from the snares of fundamentalism. Yet his denial of Christian sociology is not just a reaction to fundamentalism. It is also evidence of a basic assumption in his theoretical perspective that must be taken into account in any critical assessment of his work. And so we also consider this assumption as an active belief that shapes the formulation and exposition of his latter-day pluralism theory.

I focus my reaction on Berger's comment that "There cannot be Christian sociology, any more than Christian chemistry or Christian automotive engineering." Although he puts this statement in brackets, I do not read it as incidental or parenthetical. It represents a recurring element in his scientific and theoretical understanding of our social "secularity."[2] This idea therefore demands a critical assessment of how such a proscription functions within his overall sociological perspective, for it is evident again and again when reading his carefully crafted statements. If Berger's essay is to be taken seriously by scholars who consider that our status as bearers of the divine image in God's creation cannot be "bracketed," then a Christian critical confrontation with this statement will have to somehow locate itself within an appraisal of Berger's positive contributions to sociology and broader scientific scholarship, while at the same time rejecting the bracketed material.

In *Invitation to Sociology*, "Faith in a Pluralist Age," and other writings, Berger cheerfully accepts that those engaged in sociological research should be prepared to challenge taken-for-granted myths that hide or blur the relationships that constitute some social reality. Such an exposé is sensitive to the social context in which the social scientific observer finds him or herself. Accordingly, in "Faith in a Pluralist Age," we read that it took Berger nearly twenty years of professional scientific involvement in sociology to accept that his adherence to "secularization theory" flew in the face

---

2. We do not forget that "bracketing" is an important feature of Berger's "phenomenological" sociology. See Berger and Luckmann, *Social Construction*, 8, 26, 34, 210.

of empirical reality. This admission makes Berger's sociological observations intriguing and challenging within the academic world, particularly in North America. He openly recognizes his own ambivalence.[3]

By drawing attention to this paradigm shift, Berger confirms the ethic of stringent honesty with which he has sought to confront social reality. Our problem as Christian scholars, then, is to give due consideration to the context of Berger's contribution even while raising our dissent. Pluralism has appeared in Berger's writings before.[4] I do not disagree with the observation that our "secularity" or "secular society" is inherently pluralist, but my experience and my theoretical orientation combine to challenge Berger's rejection of a Christian sociology. Perhaps we should ask Berger his own question—"Says who?"—in our attempt to gain a critical understanding not just *that* there is no Christian sociology, but also *how* this is so. We might also, somewhat provocatively, note his own warning about uncritically accepting someone's change in attitude simply because that person has said so.[5]

"Faith in a Pluralist Age" contains themes that are present in Berger's publications all the way back to 1954.[6] This latest piece requires us to study it carefully, giving each statement he makes the attention it deserves. It is written to be read and studied and no doubt will be, along with numerous recent interviews. With Berger's ideas in mind, I will share my own reflections, which will reveal something of what I understand to be a Christian sociology of knowledge that takes seriously our calling as God's

---

3. Smelser, "Rational and Ambivalent," 1–16. Interestingly, Smelser's highly reflective ASA presidential address of 1997 does not cite Berger even if rational choice theory might be considered as one possible form in which the "social construction of reality" comes to expression. "Ambivalence" is a theme developed by Robert K. Merton and Elinor Barber (1963), but Berger's ability to searchingly criticize his own formulations has served to alert sociologists to an inherent "ambivalence" within the sociological perspective—he refers to this as "alternation." Berger, "Digression: Alternation and Biography."

4. See Berger and Luckmann, "Secularization and Pluralism," 73–84.

5. Berger, *Invitation*, 80. The full quotation reads: "The sociological perspective, with its irritating interjection of the question 'Says who?' into the grand debate of *Weltanschauungen*, introduces an element of sober skepticism that has an immediate utility in giving some protection at least against converting too readily." There is a scholarly question here concerning how Berger's earlier compliance with "secularization theory" was manifest in his writing and that also requires investigation. His own retrospective view, bolstering his "pluralism theory," needs systematic textual confirmation.

6. Berger, "Sectarianism," 467–85.

image-bearers "to live at the center of a kaleidoscope of ever-changing roles."[7] My aim is to encourage scholarly communication across different perspectives and commitments, particularly between those who do not see any possibility for a Christian sociology and those who do. Along the way I hope I can contribute useful questions about how social research should confront our complex differentiated social reality. Following Berger's own concern about fundamentalism, I hope also to stimulate a much greater level of self-critical social awareness among Christian students, including those who have to deal with the cultural consequences of Christian initiatives driven by a fundamentalist outlook.

My Path to a Christian Sociology

My confrontation with the sociological works of Peter Berger goes back to my undergraduate years at Monash University (1969–1971). While there I "discovered" my vocation as a Christian student. For as long as I have been reading works of sociology, I have had to negotiate the very claim that Berger makes in "Faith in a Pluralist Age"—that there is no Christian sociology. Berger was not, however, the first Christian writer I read who affirmed this view; it was already promoted back then to some extent by evangelical and other Christian academics as well as student leaders at the university.

Berger's *Invitation to Sociology* was listed in the Arts Faculty Handbook as "Preliminary Reading" for sociology. Once I read it, it took a few years for the full implications of Berger's perspective to sink in. But at the beginning of my third year, in a course on the Sociology of Education, I came to realize that our lecturer's insistence that sociology is a secular and religiously neutral discipline was not a research finding, but a pre-scientific postulate which he took for granted—and with which I could not agree. If there were to be no room for a scientific or theoretical contribution from the standpoint of a Christian worldview, this then rendered my own participation in such an enterprise as highly problematic. This insight hit like a bombshell.

It happened in this way. In the Sociology of Education course, Peter Berger and Thomas Luckmann's *The Social Construction of Reality: A Treatise in the Sociology of Knowledge* was presented not only as a text for understanding schooling and university education, but for understanding

---

7. Berger, *Invitation*, 62.

sociology *per se*. Our lecturer affirmed this in words that I have not forgotten: "My view is this," he said. "Life is basically meaningless until we, as human actors, create meaning for ourselves. Life is meaningless and sociology is the study of how we create meaning." This idea, I took it, explained in a nutshell *The Social Construction of Reality*. Of course, I could have questioned whether the lecturer's statement truly represented the nuanced viewpoint of Berger and Luckmann. Taken on its own, without verification by analysis of Berger and Luckmann's argument, it surely seemed to endorse an existentialist, even nihilist, viewpoint. But we were repeatedly advised against getting "bogged down" in philosophical abstractions. We were "doing sociology," after all!

Later, I was able to connect that lecturer's statement, and its impact upon me, to Berger's subsequent self-critical, even self-deprecating, statement in the preface to *A Rumor of Angels*. Here, he retrospectively makes a "confession" about his earlier 1967 volume *The Sacred Canopy: Elements of a Sociological Theory of Religion*:

> I have been trained in a sociological tradition shaped by Max Weber, and so I have tried, to the best of my ability, to keep my statements "value-free." The result was a theoretical work that, quite apart from the technical jargon in which it had to be presented, read like a treatise on atheism, at least in parts.[8]

Berger realized that a possible misperception of his intention had arisen for readers of his work. Intentionally or not, a secularized viewpoint (in the teaching of sociology as in any other science) is a proposition that requires theoretical reflection particularly when presented as the true and only way to open-minded, rational, and tolerant enquiry.

As a Christian student and an office-bearer in the Monash Evangelical Union (EU), and as organizer of a substantial network of cell-groups across the campus, this bombshell confronted me with a series of problems quite apart from its challenge to my coursework. The light may have been turned on in the lecture theater but it somehow kept shining outside in everyday life.

Alongside these intellectual challenges from the field of sociology there was the persistent impact of the apologetics of Francis Schaeffer. At that time, I was well versed in *Escape from Reason*,[9] having read it during

---

8. Berger, *Rumor*, ix.
9. Schaeffer, *Escape*.

high school days. This work represented Schaeffer's more apolitical, "co-belligerent" phase, a decade before he wrote the *Christian Manifesto*[10] and became a leading voice for the Moral Majority. It is noteworthy that in *Escape from Reason*, Schaeffer mentions the spiritual relevance of the post-structuralist and postmodern perspectives of Foucault; that was some time before Foucault became fashionable.[11] The other major intellectual authority among EU students was John Stott, whose *Basic Christianity*[12] was evangelical orthodoxy. Stott challenged the anti-intellectualism that was leading to fundamentalist activism among evangelical groups.[13]

Looking back on that lecture in the Sociology of Education course, I assume the lecturer was attempting to put a summary proposition before us as we considered the Berger and Luckmann volume in relation to the Sociology of Education sub-discipline. He was seeking to be a good teacher, pointing us to the work's leading idea. But in so doing, he also brought me to a fork in the road: was I, as a Christian, going to take the student vocation seriously or not? In so doing, he forced me to confront whether this statement—"Life is basically meaningless"—can be squared with a Christian worldview. Should I drop out of the course? If I did, what would it mean to take a stance on a Christian worldview in that context? My irritation peaked in that moment, but from that peak a fresh perspective emerged. My more mature housemate, a fellow sociology student who was the EU president, gave me good advice when he said, "If you don't confront this view head on, who is going to do so?"

Looking back, I see that what that Sociology of Education lecturer provoked, over the space of a few days, was a turning point in my own education. The root issue I was compelled to explore concerned the meaning of the Christian student vocation. "Bringing every thought captive to Christ" (2 Corinthians 10:5) took on fresh significance. The term *meaning*, despite philosophical disputation all the way from Plato to Heidegger, and the inevitable rolling of eyes by fellow Christians more concerned with being practical, could no longer be taken as a religiously neutral signifier! Language itself holds together with all things in Christ (Colossians 1:17). A new sense of what the Bible gives us began to emerge.

---

10. Schaeffer, *Christian Manifesto*.
11. Schaeffer, *Escape*, 69–71.
12. Stott, *Basic Christianity*.
13. See also Stott, *Christ the Controversialist: A Study in Some Essentials of Evangelical Religion*.

Sometime later, this lecturer suggested that by taking his comment so seriously, I was in danger of becoming "hung up" on philosophy. Yet for me, at least, he had performed an act of profound social, sociological, and even philosophical significance. By his pre-scientific comment, he not only made room for his own deeply held view, but also opened up a space within social scientific discourse in which students were invited to take seriously their own sense of personal responsibility as they gave formal expression to what they were learning in coursework.

Alternative

So I began to see university study differently. A BA qualifies a graduate to be a student; a Christian BA is a student who is called to be actively and responsibly at work in study *coram Deo* ("in the presence of God"). I had not hitherto grasped this notion, despite having immersed myself in the perspectives of Schaeffer and Stott and many others. From that point on, my vocational commitment was to contribute as a student to the development of a Christian sociology rather than to a humanistic sociology that claimed "religious neutrality."

Around this time I met Ted Fackerell, who was teaching mathematics. (He subsequently became a recognized authority in applied mathematics, quantum physics and black hole research.) At the time we met he had recently returned to Australia from Caltech. Knowing full well that some find it outrageous, Ted insisted that there is indeed a "Christian view of the State." He also said it is quite permissible to affirm a "Christian mathematics," a "Christian physics," and, for that matter, a "Christian sociology." But there was always a self-critical philosophical rider: as a Christian you had better first know what you are talking about, since the reputation of the Person you claim to be representing is involved! Philosophical reflection is therefore unavoidable in all the sciences.

Ted pointed me to the Christian philosophical work of Herman Dooyeweerd, a scholar whose name I had never heard. Dooyeweerd's four-volume *A New Critique of Theoretical Thought*[14] was housed next to Kant in the Monash University library and gave a Christian philosophical rationale for such an "outrageous" view of science. Ted said that if I were serious about a Christian sociology then I should study this work intensely, as well as the current literature of my discipline.

14. Dooyeweerd, *New Critique*, Vol. 1, 37.

The important piece of advice that Ted gave me was that as a student in *that* lecture, in *that* course, I had a responsibility to clarify what the lecturer had actually said, and what kind of statement it represents. What Ted stressed was not only about justifying one's dissent; it was that it is critical to apply what Dooyeweerd calls a "transcendental critique of theoretical thought." In Dooyeweerd's words, this is "a critical inquiry (respecting no single so-called theoretical axiom) into the universally valid conditions which alone make theoretical thought possible, and which are required by the immanent structure of this thought itself."[15]

I realized that theoretical analysis had to remain part of my scientific coursework. If I could no longer endorse the pre-theoretical grounds of non-Christian scientific contribution, neither could I require a philosophical opponent to accept the pre-theoretical religious grounds of my scientific contribution. Openly naming these assumptions made communication possible. This was not the apologetics of Francis Schaeffer, who never mentioned Dooyeweerd in his writings, and it opened up my thinking. Ultimately, what I learned from Ted's advice and Dooyeweerd's philosophy was about myself in the academic vocation. As Christian students who dissent from the view of the impossibility of a Christian sociology, we cannot simply make yet another appeal to our individual rights to free expression. Instead, our calling involves an immanent critical orientation that seeks to contribute positively to scholarly discourse. This is particularly the case when discussion involves theoretical and philosophical disagreement over pre-scientific, supra-theoretical commitments that are unavoidable in any and all scientific investigation. Even when axioms with alleged self-evidence are set forth—as with what I had heard in that 1971 Sociology of Education lecture, or with the bracketed comment in Berger's lead essay in this book—our reply needs to be part of a bold and comprehensive scientific communication. Scientific discourse is not autonomous and self-sufficient. To defend the distinctive integrity of normative scientific discourse, as well as Christian faith, one must distinguish clearly between theoretical argument and supra-theoretical pre-judgments about the meaning and purpose of science within human responsibility.[16] Christian scholarship seeks to expose the dogmatic myth of scientific and religious neutrality.[17]

---

15. Ibid., 37.
16. Ibid., 70.
17. Clouser, *Religious Neutrality*.

Peter Berger studies

Berger is certainly right to point to the change in climate concerning secularization theory. But we should add that when secularization theory was in vogue (as when I was an undergraduate student in the 1970s), it was affirmed by a plurality of sociological perspectives in diverse philosophical ways, from structural-functionalist theory (Parsons and Merton) to interactionism (various Weberian derivatives) to conflict theory, critical theory, and Marxism. Sociology endorsed pluralism within its own bounds. It was simply assumed that secularization had pushed religion to the margins of public and professional life. As a result, for many, there was no question of whether there could be a distinctively Christian sociology. It was assumed that religion meant nothing more than social involvement in a church or church institutions, and that the modern Christian should give religion a thorough and long overdue makeover by taking seriously the principles of autonomous human personality.

There are good reasons why Peter Berger's contribution to sociology has inspired critical analysis and the careful appropriation of his insights. (In Australia and New Zealand, where American sociology has had an enduring impact, successive generations of university students in the social sciences, history, and the humanities have been directed to, and inspired by, his work.)

Berger's work has encouraged students to take their own social perspectives seriously in their professionally oriented coursework. Furthermore, Berger's scholarship has been a positive stimulus to Christians in their post-university professional work, having alerted them to important, ironic, and overlooked facets of our emerging societal complexity worldwide. Critical engagement with such a stimulating Christian thinker can be very rewarding scientifically and for faith.

But the critical point of any Christian sociological contribution to Berger studies is not necessarily to accommodate the postulate that Christian sociology is impossible. Rather, critical examination of how this postulate functions in his scientific contribution should lead to an articulated theoretical account of the differentiated structures of human societal responsibility. In that context the study of the plurality of societal structures will also confront the diverse ways of life that Berger seeks to capture in his pluralist theory of contemporary religions.

Conclusion

In conclusion, let us consider further comments from Berger that must have a bearing on our critical interpretation of his proscription of a "Christian sociology":

> My meta-scientific presuppositions...have religious rather than philosophical roots. From time to time I have had a bad conscience about this and with it the feeling that I ought, as it were, to clean up my act philosophically. I have not found it possible to do so. There are only so many things one can do and this, it seems, is not going to be one of them.[18]

In a discussion of human institutions, Berger notes a crucial difference between animal and human conduct. Animals are channeled by their instincts. Not so for humans. For humans to say "I have no choice" is self-deceit.

> Their institutional character may be the only identity they can imagine having, with the alternative seeming to them as a jump into madness. This does not change the fact that the statement "I must" is a deceptive one in almost every social situation.[19]

Yet, is not Berger's bracketed denial of Christian sociology presented to us in these "I must" terms? And yet, following Arnold Gehlen and Jean-Paul Sartre, Berger identifies "bad faith" as the pretense that something is necessary that in fact is voluntary. Humans have a penchant for preferring explanations that claim an inevitable restriction on their personal choices.[20] If Berger can recognize the deceit of the "institutional imperative" in almost every social situation, why does he not recognize it in this one? The bracketed comment we have dealt with would seem to suggest that this is his own "of course" statement.[21] That there cannot be a Christian sociology is presented as a self-evident and unproblematic axiom. I am not suggesting that a Christian sociology is unproblematic; but to assert its impossibility is highly contentious, *even on his own terms*. The ironic point of my dissent is that the manner in which Berger has put this proscription forward actually *invites* dissent even if he finds it difficult, if not impossible, to dispose of

---

18. Berger, "Epilogue," 223–24.
19. Berger, *Invitation*, 164.
20. Ibid., 164–65.
21. Ibid., 60.

such a dogmatic postulate about the academic field in which he has labored for so many years.

We may detect an underlying unwillingness to debunk his own "of course" statements here, but we need to concede he has also handed his readers the weapons for such critique. The fact that it is stated *en passant* might suggest the view that he has sidestepped the possibility of de-bunking. The statement in brackets has theoretical implications, but is he going to assert that it is an empirically verifiable necessity for social scientific engagement? At this point, to repeat, we credit Berger's own open, self-critical admission of a bad conscience. Such self-criticism in Berger's writings prompts dissenters to freely disagree with him on this point. Whatever else it needs, Christian sociology will benefit from insights that arise from an immanent critique of Berger's sociology, including exploration of his rationale for his bracketed denial, giving due respect to his reflexive self-debunking as enduring features of his scholarship.

In other words, Christian sociological scholarship will need to deepen its philosophical appreciation for the challenge posed by his denial of its possibility, even as he affirms his Christian faith. This requires the cultivation of a truly critical awareness. Other scholars who share Berger's sociological outlook do not give much attention to this denial. Perhaps for them, the possibility of a Christian sociology has simply not arisen as an issue on their secularized theoretical horizon. Perhaps it is so taken-for-granted it simply needs no comment, let alone justification. That presumption will also be challenged when a careful philosophical analysis confronts this denial in a contribution to Berger studies.

I have given voice to one central concern I have with Berger's lead essay. Christian dissent from the bracketed comment must emphasize several points. Those of us who embrace the possibility of a Christian sociology—and recognize that acknowledging this possibility can make an authentic contribution to sociology—cannot merely adopt Berger's standpoint. We must proceed to clean up our own philosophical act. In his frank and public statement about *his* bad conscience, Berger has not only recognized the limits of his own contribution, but has also set an example for self-critical reflection in the discipline. This is also apparent in his suggestion of a limit to his own competence, and hence we should see in this act an implicit recognition of the necessary division of labor within the scientific enterprise. If sociology is to flourish there is work to do on many fronts.

A contribution to Berger studies from the standpoint of a Christian sociology should refrain from accepting Berger's frank admission as merely an "of course" statement, a postulate that is dogmatically above and beyond criticism. We should not avoid the difficult scholarly labor that is involved in the complex philosophical dimensions of sociological research. And so we move on past rhetorical critique (such as "Debunker, debunk thyself!") to analysis of Berger's thought in its entirety, and of its underlying presuppositions—penetrating to the religious roots of his sociological perspective, and challenging the ambiguities in its philosophical grounding.

Bibliography

Berger, Peter L. "Digression: Alternation and Biography." In *Invitation to Sociology: A Humanistic Perspective*, ch. 3. Ringwood, Australia: Pelican, 1968, 68–80.

———. "Epilogue." In *Making Sense of Modern Times: Peter L. Berger and the Vision of Interpretive Sociology*, edited by J. D. Hunter and S. C. Ainlay, 221–35. London: Routledge and Kegan Paul, 1986.

———. *Invitation to Sociology: A Humanistic Perspective*. Ringwood, Australia: Pelican, 1968.

———. *A Rumor of Angels: Modern Society and the Rediscovery of the Supernatural*. Garden City, NY: Doubleday, 1967.

———. *The Sacred Canopy: Elements of a Sociological Theory of Religion*. Garden City, NY: Doubleday, 1969.

———. "The Sociological Study of Sectarianism." *Social Research* 21 (1954) 467–85.

Berger, Peter L., and Thomas Luckmann. "Secularization and Pluralism." *International Yearbook for the Sociology of Religion* 2.2 (1966) 73–84.

———. *The Social Construction of Reality: A Treatise in the Sociology of Knowledge*. Ringwood, Australia: Penguin, 1975.

Clouser, Roy A. *The Myth of Religious Neutrality: An Essay on the Hidden Role of Religious Belief in Theories*. Revised ed. Notre Dame, IN: University of Notre Dame Press, 2005.

Dooyeweerd, Herman. *A New Critique of Theoretical Thought*. 4 vols. Amsterdam: H. J. Paris, 1955–1958.

Merton, Robert K. and Elinor Barber. "Sociological Ambivalence." In *Sociological Theory, Values, and Sociocultural Change*, edited by E. A. Tiryakian, 91–120. New York: Free Press, 1963.

Schaeffer, Francis A. *A Christian Manifesto*. Wheaton, IL: Crossway, 1982.

———. *Escape from Reason*. Leicester, UK: InterVarsity, 1968.

Smelser, Neil J. "The Rational and the Ambivalent in the Social Sciences." *American Sociological Review* 63 (1998) 1–16.

Stott, John R.W. *Basic Christianity*. Leicester, UK: InterVarsity, 1958.

———. *Christ the Controversialist: A Study in Some Essentials of Evangelical Religion*. London: Tyndale, 1970.

3

Maintaining Christian Consistency in a Pluralist Context

by Roger E. Olson

Foy Valentine Professor of Christian Theology and Ethics
George W. Truett Seminary of Baylor University
Waco, Texas

As a Christian theologian I find myself in *near* complete agreement with Peter Berger's arguments in this essay. The same is true of his book *The Many Altars of Modernity*, which he references near the beginning of this essay. I have come to know Berger late in both our lives and I cherish our friendship. I was amazed and flattered when he asked me to lunch for conversation and then invited me to respond to his book in a colloquium, and now to this essay, which says essentially what he said in the book.

I have no argument with the main descriptive points in this essay and in the book. We Christians, and people of other persuasions, live together in pluralism and must find ways to co-exist peacefully. Pluralism as peaceful co-existence is good for everyone. I belong to a Christian tradition that has always, from its very beginnings, cherished and promoted religious freedom and non-intervention, non-coercion in religion and conscience by states. (I consider myself at least an Anabaptist wannabe and definitely a "baptist" with James McClendon's small "b"—encompassing many more than churches and denominations of the big "B" variety.)

In fact, the only quarrel I have with Berger's argument is over a point only hinted at in this essay but more fully explored and promoted in the book. In this essay Berger puts it this way: "*If secular spaces are to be allowed in society, they must be allowed in individual consciousness.* Put differently, if the First Amendment (separation of church and state) is to function in American society, there must be its miniaturized version in the minds of citizens." In *The Many Altars of Modernity* Berger referred to this proposal as the "internalization of secular discourse" in religious, even Christian, minds.

In other words, if I understand Berger correctly, pluralism—more specifically, the peaceful co-existence of different worldviews and religions—will only function *if* and *insofar as* religious people internalize secular discourse and operate in parts of their lives as if God does not exist (*etsi Deus non daretur*). According to Berger, Hugo Grotius, one of my heroes (as an Arminian Protestant!), pioneered in this with his work on international law. I cannot read Grotius's mind, of course, but I question whether he internalized secular discourse or even personally operated as if God does not exist. I will return to that later.

Berger speculates about the famous Christian mystic Teresa of Avila and about Pope Francis to further illustrate what he means by internalizing secular discourse in a religious mind. Surely, he suggests, Teresa examined the financial accounts of the Carmelite convents while not in the throes of spiritual ecstasy. Similarly, Berger suggests, Pope Francis does not call an exorcist when the "popemobile" won't start; he calls a mechanic. Again, as with Grotius, I question whether these are examples of internalizing secular discourse in Christian minds. Perhaps something else is going on in these and similar cases.

Let me state my own belief about the proper functioning of "the Christian mind" and then return to my reasons for suggesting that the case studies Berger mentions may not be what he thinks they are. Berger also mentions the great Dutch theologian and statesman Abraham Kuyper. Probably Kuyper's best known quote is "There is not a square inch in the whole domain of our human existence over which Christ, who is Sovereign over all, does not cry, Mine!" Surely he also meant that Christ claims as his own every thought of the Christian's mind. By "square inch" Kuyper did not mean, of course, literal geography; he meant aspect, feature, realm, sphere. I agree with Kuyper about this—as every Christian should!

So, as my students would say, what gives here? How can what Peter says about Kuyper be true, and this famous axiom be his as well? I believe that in his "spheres of sovereignty" theology and political ethic, Kuyper was not internalizing secularity; he was operating out of a mind filled with the mercy, tolerance, and love of Christ. He knew, as the Anabaptists did before him, that Jesus Christ, unlike many Christian thinkers and authorities of Christendom, did not intend to dominate everyone or coerce them to obey him. Following Christ's example of permitting people to accept or reject him, Kuyper set up a social order that avoided requiring people to accept Christianity. But that does not mean it was thereby not a Christian social order! It was not a Christian social order by the standards of Christendom, but so what? From a free church perspective Christendom never was, and still is not, Christian!

When I, as an American Christian, agree wholeheartedly with my Baptist spiritual ancestors about separation of church and state, I am not internalizing secularity. I am protecting my faith from government interference and following Christ, as I understand him, in permitting people to worship other lords or none. I am making room for faith rather than force. That's Christian, even if not Christendom. It isn't secularity at work within me. To an outsider, someone who cannot read my mind or heart, it may appear secular, but I know it's not. I am for separation of church and state for Christian reasons—as I and my faith tradition understand Christianity.

When the radical reformers of the sixteenth century, the Anabaptists among them, called for freedom of religion and non-interference by the state in religion and conscience, they were not internalizing secularity. They were working out the implications of their fresh but faithful understanding of the New Testament. Unlike the magisterial reformers, the radical reformers believed in free will. They believed that people should come to Christ by their own free will, not under compulsion or threat. That's how they read the New Testament. By no means were they accommodating to pluralism or internalizing secularity! A modern sociologist studying them might be tempted to think they were doing just those things; anyone who has read their own arguments against Christendom, however, knows better. All their reasons are drawn from Scripture.

To state my view rather baldly, without ornamentation: A Christian ought never to internalize secular discourse even though to a secular person who cannot read the Christian's mind it might appear that he or she is doing just that. One important task of Christian discipleship is to bring every thought "captive to Christ" (2 Corinthians 10:5). Secularity is foreign to Christianity except insofar as it means making space around oneself for others to be different—accepting pluralism. But to the consistent Christian, pluralism is inevitable until the Kingdom of God appears. And, as Berger argues, it has earthly benefits insofar as it is the byproduct of freedom of religion (including freedom for non-religion).

Let me return now to the examples Berger offers of internalized secularity in highly religious, even devoutly Christian, people. It appears to me that Berger is assuming that "religious discourse" necessarily includes ecstatic and/or supernatural experiences. This is wrong. Christian theology includes something called "general providence"—God working through natural causes that he himself has established as part of creation. It also includes reason as part of the image of God in the human person.

The problem with Berger's illustration of Teresa of Avila switching, as it were, to secularity when examining the financial records of the Carmelite convents is that for Teresa—as for most informed Christians—mathematics is rooted in God, and using mathematical skills is using God-given reason. Examining the financial records of convents is not secular; it also isn't ecstatic. Religion may include mystical ecstasy, but mystical ecstasy is not the only religious state of experience—according to Christian theology. One cannot read Teresa's mind as she examines "the books," and contrasting her mode of experience then as compared with her ecstatic states, it may appear that she has switched off "religion" and switched on "secularity." But that isn't necessarily the case at all! For her, one may assume, "religion," even Christianity, was not confined to her mystical ecstasies. It included everything she did. Or, to put it another way, everything she did was saturated with her Christian beliefs. For her, almost without doubt, mathematics was rooted in God and the ability to reason mathematically was part of the image of God.

Now, of course, for the Christian person, none of that is on the surface, where it would be obvious and visible to the non-Christian mind. So, it's understandable that an observer who doesn't understand the consistent Christian mind might conclude, wrongly, that the supernatural and ecstatic is somehow the religious part of a Christian mystic's life and that doing mathematics and bookkeeping is the secular part of her life. But to Teresa that was, hopefully, not the case. It certainly does not need to be the case.

What about Pope Francis and the uncalled-for exorcist? In Peter's illustration, the popemobile won't start. Does the fact that he (or his assistant) calls a mechanic instead of an exorcist reveal that a part of his mind is operating as if God does not exist? Does that mean he has internalized secularity? Of course, I can't read the Pope's mind, but I will dare to argue that relying on an auto mechanic rather than an exorcist reveals nothing about one's inner thoughts or beliefs.

I grew up in a Pentecostal context, a religious form of life in which people commonly did both: they prayed *and* called a mechanic when their vehicles broke down. However, most people did not see anything wrong with relying on an auto mechanic to fix their cars, even if they thought it good to pray as well. Now I participate in a religious form of life (Baptist) in which very few people would think to pray for their car to start; instead, most automatically call a mechanic. Does that mean Baptists internalize secularity to a greater extent than Pentecostals? It would seem so to an outside observer. It might seem so to some Pentecostals! However, I do not think that is necessarily the case.

Since Berger uses some lighthearted and even entertaining stories to illustrate his point, I'll dare to use one I often heard growing up in church. According to the probably apocryphal sermon illustration, a man was stranded on his roof during a terrible flood. He cried out to God to save him from drowning as the water inched higher and higher. Along came a man in a rowboat who offered to rescue the man on the roof. The praying man said, "No thank you. God is going to answer my prayer and rescue me." But the water kept creeping closer, so the man on the roof cried out more desperately, "God, please save me from drowning!" Along came another boat whose rower offered to take the praying man to safety. Again, the praying man declined. The same thing happened again. Finally, as the water engulfed the man and he began to drown he shouted, "God, why didn't you save me?" God finally spoke, and said, "I tried. I sent you three boats."

That sermon illustration was meant to caution super-spiritual Christians against refusing natural means and prudence to be well and succeed in life. It was never intended to discourage praying, of course. The point was that the Christian man on the roof should have regarded the first boat that came along as an answer to his prayer. Now, had the man accepted one of the offers by the boatmen, an unbelieving neighbor—or even a believing sociologist of religion—might have thought, "Oh, look, he's being secular now. He stopped praying and got into a boat." But certainly from the Christian's perspective that's not at all the case.

My point here is simply that, to a Christian mind, making prudent use of seemingly natural laws, events, and opportunities does not constitute thinking or acting "as if God does not exist." Christians have always believed God acts through secondary causes including natural laws, events, and opportunities.

In *The Many Altars of Modernity* Berger argues that in order to fly an airplane a pilot must internalize secularity. I argue that's not the case. A Christian pilot presumably believes God is the author of natural laws, nature's regularities, and of our human abilities to study and understand them and make use of them. The "background belief" there is general providence. The Christian pilot, hopefully, is flying the plane for the glory of God and the good of neighbors. Hopefully he is also praying at least occasionally that God will help him fly the plane well. According to good Christian theology there is no need for him to switch back and forth "on the ground" (at church) and "in the air" (flying the plane) between religious and secular discourse. Both natural and supernatural are under God's sovereignty. His inner discourse can and should be all of one piece.

I think what Berger is assuming is that "the religious" includes only what is mystical, ecstatic, and/or supernatural. For Christians it shouldn't only include those. Even the natural falls within the realm of the religious in that its creator, maker, and lord is God. Natural laws are viewed as regularities of God's continuing creativity. Humans' ability to rely on and use them also comes from God. And all uses of them should be to the glory of God and for one's neighbors' good.

Now, admittedly, not all of that is on the fully conscious level of most Christians' minds. And it may be that some Christians—perhaps many—have succumbed to a dualism that places a partition in their minds between the "natural" and the "religious." My point is simply that Christians can operate in the world, making use of modern technology, studying nature, getting along with non-Christians—without internalizing competing discourses about what is natural and what is religious. And I would be willing to bet that the Pope does not think he is internalizing secular discourse when he has his assistants call a mechanic to fix the popemobile.

Acknowledging that I could be wrong and perhaps have misunderstood Berger (but I don't think so), I will now explain what mistake I think underlies his analysis and proposal. It seems to me that Berger is assuming that religious discourse is always tied to something supernatural, and is incompatible with acceptance of disagreement (pluralism). And it seems to me he is assuming that what he calls "secularity" is neutral with regard to worldviews, ideologies, and religions.

Maintaining Christian Consistency in a Pluralist Context

As I have explained, however, traditional Christianity is not tied solely to supernatural experiences and expectations. Traditional Christianity includes them but is not reducible to them. Traditional Christianity accepts the natural—as part of God's general providence and sovereignty. Therefore, a Christian can engage in, for example, "methodological atheism" in experimental science while at the same time thinking, "The natural laws, causes, events and processes I'm studying belong to God." For the Christian a better phrase than "methodological atheism" would be "methodological naturalism." It does not exclude God but neither does it look for supernatural explanations or call on God to intervene. In Christian theology, with its doctrine of general providence, that stance is perfectly consistent with belief in God as creator and sovereign lord. One is not acting "as if God does not exist" but only "as if the supernatural does not exist"—here, at this moment, in this experimental science investigation. The "as if" is important and often overlooked.

Furthermore, one could argue that secularity is itself not really ideologically neutral.[1] Secularity asks the Christian to set aside his or her belief in God's sovereign lordship over every inch of creation, and to pretend that God does not exist. That's asking the Christian to deny his or her belief in God. For the Christian, bracketing God "out" even in one part of life is the same as denying God. The ancient Romans persecuted Christians because they would not even pretend to believe in other gods. Secularity, especially the "internalization of secular discourse," amounts to asking the Christian to pretend not to believe in God. That internal dualism is inconsistent with the call of God to acknowledge him and his lordship over all.

The solution to the competition between religion and pluralism—or at least between Christianity and pluralism—is not for the Christian to internalize secularity. It is for the Christian to accept natural law as part of God's general providence (which is already part of traditional Christian doctrine!) and to accept people's free rejection of God as permitted by God himself. The solution also includes non-Christians, whether religious or secular, accepting that all discourses are permitted in pluralism, including Christian discourse.

---

1. See Clouser, *Myth*.

Bibliography

Berger, Peter L. *The Many Altars of Modernity: Toward a Paradigm for Religion in a Pluralist Age*. New York: De Gruyter, 2014.

Clouser, Roy A. *The Myth of Religious Neutrality*. Notre Dame, IN: University of Notre Dame Press, 2005.

4

Faith and Politics in a Pluralist Age

by Paul A. Brink

Professor of Political Science
Gordon College
Wenham, Massachusetts

The relation between religion and politics is a perennial concern in American political life, and the conversation today remains as lively and dynamic as it has ever been. While the specific topics of discussion have changed over time, headlines today continue to be dominated by debates concerning religion, and especially concerning the public face of religion, even in the opening decades of the twenty-first century. That fact in itself is testament to Peter Berger's conclusion, now nearly twenty years old, that secularization has in fact not supplanted religion, as many had predicted.[1] Rather, while the modern circumstances in which religion and religious people find themselves have changed, sometimes in dramatic ways, religion remains alive and well in America and, indeed, in most places in the world.

Recently, Berger has begun to consider these modern circumstances in greater detail. Although it is true that religion has not been pushed to the margins of either our consciousness or our societies, it has not been immune to change. More accurately, as the modern world has changed, religion has changed with it—sometimes reluctantly, occasionally enthusiastically. And of these changes, none is likely to be more significant than the plural situation in which religions find themselves: "We don't live in a secular age," writes Berger, "We live in a pluralist age." And so Berger has

---

1. Berger, *Desecularization*.

begun to explore the reality that we now live in societies in which many religions can be found in close proximity to one another. In *The Many Altars of Modernity* (2014), as well as in the essay that opens this volume, Berger has begun to develop a theory of pluralism that can replace the now-discredited theory of secularization.

Berger's goal is precisely on point. We desperately need theories that are adequate to account for the changed social situation of religion. Much of Berger's discussion concerns the situation of religious people, institutions, and communities that must make sense of this strange new pluralist world. In particular, he points to the challenge raised by *secularity*, shared spaces where people work out the nuts and bolts of life together. He focuses on the challenge secularity poses to the religious, but of course the challenge is one that all participants must face, secular as well as religious. If Berger is correct that secularization fails, and that modernity admits religion, our pluralist situation is going to be a challenging one for secular people, too, and especially for those who have been true believers in the secularization thesis. Disestablishment can be a challenging process for anyone, not only for the religious!

My focus here is particularly on the *political* dimensions of the pluralist challenge. A central question in the development of a genuinely pluralist theory will concern what it may imply about the nature of the state and of politics. The sphere of political life presents unique opportunities to consider the perils and the prospects of pluralism, as it is perhaps the only area of human life explicitly dedicated to conciliating difference.

We might begin by considering what is required for politics to be possible in pluralist societies. Significantly, by *pluralism* we do not mean simply that people with different identities—religious or otherwise—are active in politics, which can make conversation difficult. It's actually a deeper sort of pluralism. It is not that we have a variety of teams competing in a great political game; rather we have basic disagreements concerning what game it is that we are playing. What are its rules? How do we define fair play? What are the goals? Of course, we inherit some political givens—guidance concerning the nature of institutions, for example, or the role of democracy, or the relationship between majorities and minorities—and while these are renegotiated and reinterpreted from time to time, they set the stage for our deliberations. Nonetheless, the debate we encounter in political life is a deep one; it concerns how we should go about doing politics itself.

Now, as Berger notes, the challenge of pluralism is not an entirely novel problem. Indeed, the reigning political philosophy today, political liberalism, grew up in the seventeenth and eighteenth centuries, partly in response to a situation not unlike our own—the fragmentation of Europe that accompanied the wars of religion. Obviously, these religious wars posed a very practical challenge for political life: How are we to govern people so willing to kill each other over matters of religion? But they also posed a tremendous theoretical challenge: When people disagree about so much that is important, upon what can we establish the authority of the state?

In that early modern era, the figure of Thomas Hobbes looms large. Hobbes is significant not merely for his attempt to tame religious conflict by accommodating it within the framework of the modern state; more than that, he initiated a major philosophical response to the challenge of pluralism more widely—a response that still is our default response today. Broadly understood, it is also the path Berger takes in the outlines of his pluralist theory.

What was that strategy? Hobbes and other early liberals set about finding foundations for the state and for law that were independent of theology—that, in Berger's language, were "without religious presuppositions." Faced with radical religious plurality, early liberals sought to establish political order on whatever else might be found that people had in common, and thereby ensure a framework in which widespread agreement on some "commonness" might enable those who disagreed on so much to live together within the same society. Hobbes is especially significant as one of the earliest to attempt to accomplish this. Berger cites Hugo Grotius as accomplishing something similar.

This approach is not unreasonable. From the time of the ancient Greeks onward, a widespread consensus on matters of morality and identity had long been understood to provide—and probably did provide—a stable foundation for peaceful society. Given the breakdown in this consensus and its frightful consequences for politics, the search for a new consensus was a natural step. This new foundation was to be uncontroversial, reliable, and uniform—true for everyone, regardless of differences of belief or other differences in identity.

It seems to me that late moderns are involved today in efforts that are similar to those of the early moderns. We might call it "the politics of abstraction": faced with disagreement, we seek to abstract from our pluralism in search of a foundation, or as Berger puts it, a "secular space" that is somehow independent of any and all religious views, and similarly independent of any other pluralisms that might threaten our stability. In other words, we, like Hobbes, are engaged in the project of finding an alternative neutral foundation for our politics.

The problem is that we are having great difficulty finding a foundation that works for us. The chief challenge is that any basis for authority robust enough to do the work required of it is bound to be controversial, and in fact privileges certain groups or perspectives over others. In our concern to establish the foundations for political order on something other than religion or any other controversial moral doctrine, we search for some even lower common denominator that can somehow unite us; freedom, reason, nature, contract, and secularism—all have been candidates at one time or another. Once the foundation is articulated and established, then any difference (cultural, religious, racial, and so on) can be "tolerated" so long as it does not violate the commonality undergirding the regime.

What is overlooked, however, is that to pursue such a strategy of "tolerance" is actually to relegate vital aspects of human identity to the realm of public indifference; they're trivialized, or recast as mere preference. It is not hard to see this taking place in Berger's articulation of "secularity" as a context in which people of varied religions, or no religion at all, can meet on common ground. Berger misses the fact that for persons of strong religious convictions, to adopt the discourse of secularity is actually to give up vital aspects of who they are. He sees one of the advantages of pluralism to be a requirement that religious people begin to distinguish between their "core" and "peripheral" beliefs—entirely missing the fact that such a requirement will offend the very people he should be most interested in inviting into the public space. This is the difficulty with the "both/and" strategy that Berger articulates. He assumes that the apparent dualism that he observes in religious people is widespread, and even more problematically, he seems to believe that it should be a requirement that religious people entering into politics or auto mechanics or accounting (or sociology!) thereby enter into a space of secularity. But Berger misses the full extent of religious pluralism. Whether or not the both/and option is appropriate, or can be accomplished, is itself a matter of religious disagreement. A good many religious people believe that their politics, their auto mechanics, their accounting (and their sociology) actually ought to be based on their religious convictions. Their religious beliefs are not only about *something other* than these things, but also about these very things!

In a similar way, Berger describes how pluralism leads people to question their own beliefs, providing "new insight" into the nature of faith—namely, the acceptance of doubt. Berger goes so far as to suggest that pluralism offers a new dimension to the meaning of *sola fide*—the acceptance of the loss of certainty that results from the relativizing effects of pluralism. But, surely, this is to beg the question; if religious people are willing to engage each other only as they come to doubt their own beliefs, the contrast between religious believers and their secular skeptics begins to break down. More helpful—and more interesting—would be a theory that sees religious people holding to orthodox and authoritative positions, yet engaging each other fully and openly in the political space. Surely it is reasonable to expect that a theory of pluralism that takes faith seriously would not depend upon faith's weakening.

Another way to consider the subject might be to focus less on the *grounds* (religious or otherwise) upon which people depend in the shared public space, and more on *what they actually say* in the space. It is not so much that religious believers—or anyone else—distinguish between their core and their peripheral beliefs in public, but rather that they believe—as a core belief—that because of the nature of the political, they may not seek to impose their religious views on other participants. This, I would argue, has less to do with the fact of pluralism per se, and more to do with commitments, rooted in faith, to democracy and to human rights.

This can appear odd to the nonbeliever, especially within societies rooted in the political liberal tradition inaugurated by Hobbes and further developed by thinkers from John Locke to John Rawls. This tradition sees democracy and human rights themselves to be liberal creations, invented in part to counter religious forces. To suggest that there might be "Christian democracy" or "Christian foundations to human rights" may surprise political liberals. But such a reaction, I would argue, is itself part of the secularization thesis that Berger rejects. What is required, in contrast, is an approach less concerned with the strong moral-religious consensus that grounds our politics, and more concerned with emphasizing the reality of pluralism in our public life. Rather than "opening up a space for secular discourse," as Berger suggests, pluralism opens up a space for *pluralist* discourse. We ought not to seek, as Grotius did, a politics "as if God did not exist," but rather seek a politics that is religiously plural, in which multiple justifications and articulations are welcome. To suggest that pluralism opens up space for a distinctively *secular* discourse is to come dangerously close to *imposing* that discourse, that is, to attempt to overcome pluralism by mere fiat.

Here's the challenge: All of us—not only the religious, not only liberals, not only the secular, not only "them," but all of us—have to put aside the assumption that a community's political life should be based on strong moral perspectives. Perhaps such a view made sense during the era of Christendom. Perhaps it made sense for Hobbes and for Grotius, who sought a new unity once Christendom was shattered. Perhaps it made sense in the years and the decades before Berger took aim at secularization theory. But even if it made sense then, it does not now.

As an illustration, we might consider the U.S. Constitution. What is the source of authority that undergirds such a document? Why do we obey the law? It is not hard to imagine many possible answers. One central opposition, for example, has been between the so-called "divine right of kings"—we might recall Romans 13—and the "general will"—we might recall Rousseau. But the point is that we should expect that in a plural society we will receive many different answers to that question.

Such are the problems of a democratic pluralist society. Berger might suggest that when we meet together in the secular space, our religious views are held in abeyance, or he might suggest that as we encounter the views of so many who disagree we will find we can abandon certain of our "peripheral" beliefs. The liberal approach more generally might be to abstract from the differences between the perspectives in favor of some deeper basis, rooted perhaps in individual freedom, upon which we can develop a principle of toleration to adjudicate between the rivals.

But must this question actually be answered publicly? Is it important that in the political agreement we call the Constitution, we find some strong moral claim concerning the authority of the document? In this debate, is it necessary for a philosophical or theological or strong moral claim to be found *right* for one of them to actually *win*? Or might it be possible that *all of them are right*?

Obviously, philosophically, theologically, or morally, this cannot be true. In fact, the various arguments are often mutually exclusive, or largely so. But politically, constitutionally, we may not need to say so. Our silence on this point offers a big advantage: we do not need to rule against people coming into our shared spaces because of the *grounds* for their views or arguments. These sorts of exclusions only increase resentment. We also avoid asking citizens to downplay their particular identities in favor of some theorized universal, or requiring them to make distinctions between their "core" and "peripheral" beliefs, requirements that, as noted above, tend to relegate these identities, and the people who hold them, to the realm of public indifference.

This does, of course, demand that we revise our understanding of the nature of a shared public space. Rather than insisting on a strong moral consensus, we are only working for an agreement to share space. We agree on a constitutional document that governs our political space, but we do not necessarily agree about why. Adopting this posture also implies loosening control, removing ourselves from the gatekeeping function that we may have thought we had or perhaps were seeking. We may find, in fact, that the reasons people hold to the principles and procedures of our political space may vary as greatly as the people do themselves.

A genuinely pluralist theory, therefore, cannot help but be a politics of risk. In this model of politics, *everyone* is disestablished—not only the church or Christianity, but also liberalism or secularism. Such an approach can work only if all involved can recognize that genuine respect for pluralism demands that Christianity, liberalism, and secularism all be denied pride of place. The shape of a pluralist politics, therefore, will not even pretend to operate within the confines (and security) of a society-wide strong moral consensus.

Is the risk too great? Perhaps, but only if we hold to the older view that says that what most fundamentally holds a political order together is citizens' ideological or other "strong" agreement about the nature of that order. If this is true, then, given the extent of our pluralism, the situation is truly alarming, and the risk is that much greater. On the other hand, this point of view may be incorrect. There may be many more things that sustain a constitution, or more broadly, a political order, most of which have little to do with strong moral consensus on questions of ideology or identity.

Here's one possibility: A basic constitutional guarantee of equal opportunity of democratic participation is more important than a prior agreement concerning the nature or the grounds of that participation. Indeed, what else is a political community, we might ask, as distinct from other forms of human community, than a structure that embraces *all* who reside in a territory, regardless of their race, their religion, gender, ethnicity, and all the other distinctions that divide? And if the state embraces all, without regard to particularities, then the emphasis should be placed on enabling all to participate, without regard to these particularities, and especially without insisting that participation follow the rules of an imposed secularity.

If we can begin to understand our political space this way, then the risk seems to recede. What is more, if groups are not excluded on the basis of their beliefs or the grounds for their arguments, new opportunities for social stability appear. We might even find that a pluralist politics is *stronger*, as different people come to agreement on particular points or conclusions or policies without a requirement to agree on the *reasons* for those points or conclusions or policies. Thus, plurality can actually represent an opportunity, rather than a weakness, when we recognize the plural bases of support as signs of widespread support for the political enterprise.

But there are no guarantees. The pluralist theory of politics that I am outlining here depends upon the beliefs and the behaviors of the actual participants in our politics, and as we look to our fellow citizens—and even more to the politicians who seek to represent them—we might experience some pessimism about the prospects for our pluralist politics. But I think there are reasons we might yet hope. Let me make a final suggestion.

While it is true that the success of our political institutions and processes under situations of pluralism might depend on the beliefs and behaviors of the participants in those institutions and processes, it is also the case that there is a history here. These dynamics did not simply drop from the sky, nor are they recreated anew with every election or meeting of congress. Rather, what we see are repeated references and appeals to commitments, norms, and rules for political behavior that, while understood differently by different perspectives, still have a way of being understood across pluralist divides. Indeed, it is upon these bases that societies can articulate very basic political rules such as majority rule, or putting aside the recourse to violence. But even beyond these basic rules, I suspect that the nature of political life as a sphere of normative discourse will itself tend to encourage the parties towards constructive dialogue and decision-making. It is worth noting, in this regard, that the reason we can imagine constitutional polities that would open up political possibilities for pluralism is because of institutions and political ideals that themselves have a history. In that sense, we can speak of political "givens" that lead us one way or another.

This suggests something of the distinctiveness of the political realm. Philosophers, theologians, and visionaries may not be fully satisfied with the sort of pluralist agreement that I suggest should characterize politics.

Although a genuinely pluralist theory will encourage all to enter into the political sphere with all their religious (or any other) particularities intact, participants cannot expect their full vision to be realized, simply because that full vision requires respect for those who disagree. This is true even for the rules of the political arena itself; in that sense, the political ground is never "settled" but continues to place demands and limitations upon the participants.

Of course, not all of life is political, and in other areas of society, the theory of pluralism will work out in different ways. Indeed, it may be that we need not *a theory* of pluralism, but *theories* of pluralism, corresponding to the healthy differentiation of society into many different arenas of human activity, each with its own purposes, structures, principles of authority—and each, very likely, with a different required response to modern pluralist realities. So the response to pluralism articulated in politics will be appropriately different from our educational, ecclesiastical, or business responses.

But when we enter into public political life and our distinctly political visions and illusions meet one another, we may be able to persuade one another of the merits of our distinctive approaches to pluralism, to the basic rules of our political engagement, to the Constitution itself—just as we may be able to persuade one another concerning more mundane political issues. This is because when we speak politically, we frequently discover that what we mean by *pluralism* or *impartiality* or *fairness* actually is similar enough to what others mean by those terms that communication, even political agreement, becomes possible. It is true that there is no guarantee. But we do not need to expect failure, and if we find ways to meet each other, then perhaps we can say we have recognized a ground for our pluralist politics that is itself genuinely pluralist.

Bibliography

Berger, Peter, ed. *The Desecularization of the World: Resurgent Religion and World Politics*. Grand Rapids: Eerdmans, 1999.

Berger, Peter. *The Many Altars of Modernity: Toward a Paradigm for Religion in a Pluralist Age*. Boston: De Gruyter, 2014.

5

Doing Justice to Diverse Ways of Life

by James W. Skillen

President (retired), Center for Public Justice
Washington, D.C.

For decades, Peter Berger has been making a singular contribution to an understanding of societies and social practices, particularly with regard to religion. Nearly twenty years ago, in *The Desecularization of the World* (Eerdmans, 1999), he introduced the theme of his lead essay in this book, contending that religions had not faded away in the twentieth century as many scholars had predicted. Religions were not suddenly springing to life from the dead; they had never died. Fading, however, was the widespread belief that modernization was driving religions to their death. What is needed now, he argues in *Many Altars*, is a more empirically adequate "theory of pluralism" to replace the failed "secularization theory." In his opening chapter in this book, he has also added a "theological reflection" focused primarily on Christian engagement, or the lack thereof, with the multireligious, multicultural world in which we live.

In the following paragraphs, I raise some questions about presuppositions underlying Berger's proposed theory of pluralism and challenge the adequacy of his proposed theory to displace secularization theory, which continues to grip the minds, habits, and institutions of people throughout the world. Finally, I introduce a normative proposal of *principled pluralism* that may contribute to the pluralist conversation.

Doing Justice to Diverse Ways of Life

Faith, Religions, Secularity, and Secularism

Today, says Berger, we live in a pluralist age, not a secular age. Pluralism poses challenges to religious faith, but ones that are different from secularism. To explain what he means, he begins by distinguishing an empirical account of social reality that is "without any religious presupposition" from the profession and practice of religious faith. As a sociologist he pursues the empirical account; as a professing Christian he offers "a theological reflection about [his] sociological findings." This duality of fact and faith demands examination.

Let's pause to ask some questions. When he says that the modern world has witnessed a "great expansion of the space allowed for secularity" in science and technology as well as in law and other areas of social life, Berger implies, empirically speaking, that our day has more secular spaces than, let's say, the time of the late medieval period of Western Christendom. Does this mean that the space for religion has shrunk even as religions have remained vital? This might be true if we assume that medieval society was thoroughly religious. But according to Berger, "religions" are and always have been distinct from "profane" life. Here he might have in mind the way medieval Christendom identified most areas of life as "secular" in contrast to the "religious" vocations of the clergy and those in religious orders. However, in that period the word *saeculum* ("secular") did not denote or connote a disconnection from God (as being "without religious presupposition"). To the contrary, it referred to natural life and non-ecclesiastical vocations of laypeople related to God by creation and the mediating grace and authority of the church. Christendom was an integrated order of society through and through. Consequently, the secular spaces of medieval Christendom were not thought of as secular in the way Berger and most moderns use the term. Might he mean, then, that the breakdown of Christendom and the loss of church dominance over society have contributed to the expansion of non-ecclesiastical vocations and activities? Berger does not give an adequate empirical account of this dissolution, nor does he discuss the change of meaning in the use of the word *secular*. He simply uses the term in the modern sense of referring to what is not related to God, or as meaning "without any religious presupposition."

Berger is correct, empirically speaking, that social life outside the church (churches) in the modern era has developed in expansive ways with the growth and differentiation of sciences and technologies, schools and universities, businesses and commerce, the arts and leisure, and much more. Yet why should we assume that those non-ecclesiastical ventures should be interpreted from a viewpoint that is without religious presuppositions? On what basis should we accept Berger's apodictic statement that "there cannot be Christian sociology, any more than Christian chemistry or Christian automotive engineering"? For Berger it is clear that Christian faith is one thing, profane life in secular spaces another. Yet that prejudgment works only if religion is predefined in a narrow, ecclesiastical way and the secular is predefined in a broad, modern way in keeping with a secularist philosophical worldview. The difference between Berger and ideologically secularist thinkers appears to be simply that he takes empirical note of the continuing vitality of ecclesiastical practices and religious discourses and makes his own profession of faith in Christ. He does not want to do away with religion altogether, as the ideological secularists want to do. Yet the way he distinguishes religion from the secular, the sacred from the profane, law from gospel, and spiritual ecstasy from secular practicality seems to me to owe a greater debt to secularism than to medieval Catholic and Protestant views of life.

For Berger the challenge for religious people of "accepting secular spaces" is learning to accept the differentiating development of social life that is no longer under the direct influence or control of the church and is therefore, in his mind, not religious. Facing that challenge, Berger suggests, need not prove too difficult for Christians and people of other faiths if they accept his understanding of the duality of faith (or religion) and secularity. This is not a matter of "*either/or* but rather of *both/and*," he says. This is the point of view from which Berger assesses and approves the work of Hugo Grotius, who led the way to a new view of law and political practice that he believed "should be developed 'as if God did not exist' (*etsi Deus non daretur*)—that is, without any religious presuppositions." Berger largely accepts Grotius' aim as necessary and legitimate in order to bring about civic peace at that time, and he is quick to assert that Grotius' proposal represents a "methodological atheism rather than a philosophical one" because, after all, Grotius was a "pious Protestant," belonging to "the more humane branch of the Dutch Reformation." Berger does not consider Grotius or himself to be ideological secularists, because neither rejected religion altogether. But Berger's sympathy with Grotius, and his view that secular space is free of religion, aligns squarely with the secularist aim of marginalizing religion by pushing it outside the public arena for the sake of civic peace.

Doing Justice to Diverse Ways of Life

Given the controlling presuppositions of his worldview, Berger misses something significant about the statement he quotes from Grotius, something that happens to be a driving force of modern life and thought: secularism's religiously deep and *non-neutral* aim to displace the entire sacred/secular worldview and way of life that characterized medieval Christendom and much of modern Catholicism and Protestantism. The gradual disintegration of Christendom came about not because non-ecclesiastical spaces expanded and ecclesiastical space narrowed in a gradual, non-contentious way. Instead, the disintegration was driven by religiously deep conflicts among Catholics, Protestants, anti-religious secularizers, nationalists, statists, and others with different visions of life as a whole. The conflicts were not narrowly theological and not limited to concerns about how to bolster civic peace.

If, along with Berger, one pre-defines sociology, chemistry, and automotive engineering as non-religious or without religious presuppositions, then of course it follows that there can be no Christian theory of such disciplines and no Christian view of secular space. But what if the word *Christian* refers to more than church institutions and theological reflection? What if it entails something comprehensive about all of life and about the meaning of the entire cosmos? According to the Bible the entire world is God's creation and, as the New Testament states, all things have been created in, through, and for the Son of God who became incarnate in Jesus Christ (John 1:1–4; Col 1:15–20; Heb 1:1–3). On that basis, why would Christians *not* seek to understand every dimension of reality and every human vocation from a biblical point of view? That would seem to follow as naturally as the desire of ideological secularists to understand every dimension of human life and society from the viewpoint of their foundational commitment, which is that nothing transcends material reality and human actions. It appears that Berger wants to stand between two views of life, believing they can work together "both/and" as long as they are distinguished. But what, then, holds the two dialectically opposed poles together?

When Berger points to Roman Catholic and Protestant efforts to develop philosophies of natural law as evidence that they share his idea of the secular, he misses the extent to which many of those philosophical efforts are grounded in a broader framework of assumptions, including the belief that all of life belongs to God. It might well be the case that Berger and a majority of Western Christians now believe there are two distinguishable—even dialectically related—realms that can be theorized and lived in separately without conflict in a congenial "both/and." But if so, we should not assume that their view of reality represents normative Christianity; neither empirical descriptions nor theological reflection can prove that to be the case. In addition, what if it could be shown that those who hold secularist beliefs hold them not as private beliefs, but as deep convictions about how to reshape society in a broad way? It is empirically evident that those holding secularist beliefs have been able to achieve some of what their ideology demands, including the reshaping of public laws, social institutions, and educational curricula: is it not obvious that many of these "reshapings" conflict with what many Christians, Muslims, and Jews believe should constitute a healthy, rational, just, and loving society?

Secular Spaces, Religions, and Pluralism

One of the things that convinces me that Berger overlooks the significance of the religiously deep roots of conflicts among lively religions and equally lively ideologies today is that after his brief mention of "secularism" near the beginning of his essay, he says nothing further about it. If he had critically evaluated the ideological worldview of secularism, I believe he would have noted that secularists do not, in fact, hold their core belief only as an article of private faith. By its very nature secularism aims to become the ordering principle of life in a very broad sense. The various branches (or denominations) of secularism are displacement ideologies: religiously deep visions of what should take the place of Christianity and other ways of life that have shaped societies extensively. The displacement aim is no less true of Lockean liberalism than of Marxism, no less true of civil-religious nationalism (in the United States and elsewhere) than of the revolutionary radicalism of ISIS. Some of secularism's branches may affirm the legitimacy of private religious belief, while other branches may want to displace all religions altogether, but all branches aim to provide a normative way of ordering life in this world that entails the tight, privatizing marginalization of religious practices and discourse wherever they remain alive.

Berger speaks about the expansion of secular space as a progressive development that Christians can accommodate by accepting the non-religious character of what transpires in that space. They can do this, he argues, by learning to distinguish between their core, nonnegotiable beliefs and beliefs that are negotiable. The latter can then be given over to "cognitive bargaining." The core belief of Judaism, he posits, is the Shema: "Hear O

Israel, the Lord is our God, the Lord is one." The core belief of Islam is the Shehada: "There is no God but Allah, and Muhammad is his messenger." And the core belief of Christian faith is "Christ is risen." These, Berger believes, can be held personally and in church-like groups as non-negotiable dogmas without interfering in the conduct of religiously neutral activities in secular spaces.

Yet this approach seems to me to misunderstand the meaning of those core beliefs. Jews', Muslims', and Christians' core beliefs stand as central pivots of comprehensive worldviews and ways of life. What Berger takes for granted in his talk of religious pluralism, therefore, is a narrowly defined confessional pluralism that can go hand in hand with acceptance of the religious neutrality of secular spaces in which all things are negotiable. But whose view of the relation of religious and secular space should control public life and guard the boundaries between the two? And going deeper, what are the grounds for accepting the distinction between religion in a narrow sense, on one side, and secular space in a broad sense, on the other? There are no religiously neutral answers to these meta-questions.

The most fundamental presuppositions (and presumptions) of Berger's argument are neither empirically verifiable nor religiously neutral. To be sure, he professes the faith of a Lutheran Christian, not that of the secularist who opposes all religion. Yet he evidently agrees with the secularist who believes that religious faith should not intrude into secular space. Despite his criticism of secularization theory, Berger still seems to believe that religious fundamentalism is the greatest threat to civic peace, and its marginalization is therefore necessary. But it seems to me (and to many others) that the gravest threats to civic peace in the twentieth and twenty-first centuries have not come from traditional religions, but from modern displacement ideologies of a religiously equivalent character. Those include Nazism, communism, secularism, ideologically radicalized Islamism, and many versions of civil-religious nationalism and imperialism.

One of the chief questions we must explore about these modern ideologies is how they regard political life and the use of force. Non-negotiable core beliefs shape one's views about how to constitute government and politics. From my point of view, and Berger's as well, I assume, a political order (or disorder) that discriminates among citizens (or mere subjects) in ways that exclude some of them altogether (even to the point of violent elimination), or that subordinates some of them to second- or third-class status, is unacceptable and unjust. Moreover, it seems clear to me that such an order is grounded in religiously deep presuppositions about human nature and the nature of a good society, presuppositions that are directly opposed to equally profound assumptions held by others. To address this matter requires more than an affirmation that confessional pluralism is better than confessional uniformity in society. For this reason, it seems to me that Berger's theory of pluralism and his theological reflection on it do not do enough to show how public justice can be done to the diversity of living religions and religiously equivalent displacement ideologies now at work in Western (and many other) societies. Publicly potent ideologies and many self-defined religions function as ways of life, not merely as ways of worship. Beyond asserting that confessional pluralism should be accepted, we need to go on to compare the political-ordering philosophies held by Jews, Christians, Muslims, Hindus, liberals, communists, nationalists, and terrorist radicals in all of their varieties and denominations.

In contrast to Berger, I believe there is no religiously or ideologically neutral view of, or way of constituting, secular space and public governance. A liberal constitution for the governance of society differs fundamentally from a communist order. A contemporary Hindu nationalist constitution is fundamentally different from an Islamic-sharia constitution. A Christian-democratic pluralist constitution is fundamentally different from a Christian-Roman imperial constitution (whether of the Eastern or Western type). Berger implies that only a "very small portion of people" see religion and secularity as essentially antagonistic, and he apparently believes that most people—or at least most Christians in the West—share his view. But I dare say that a large number of Christians, not limited to those called "fundamentalists," do not share Berger's view.

Principled Pluralism and a Just Public Order

Insofar as I have posed critical questions about Berger's presentation, I now want to suggest a more expansive approach to social and confessional diversity that might contribute to the project he has undertaken to replace secularization theory with something better and more empirically accurate. My proposal depends and builds on the following theses:

1. To deal with religious pluralism we must deal with diverse ways of life, not only diverse professions of core beliefs and religious discourses.

Doing Justice to Diverse Ways of Life

2. What Berger speaks of as "secularity" and "secular spaces" refers to a diversity of social, political, and economic institutions, including families, schools, profit-making corporations, social service agencies, art institutes and museums, and other not-for-profit organizations *as well as* governing institutions (among which are the different branches of government, bureaucracies, electoral systems, and more).

3. The church-type institution central to many faiths, along with a diverse range of self-identified religious and ideological schools, social service agencies, clubs, and other not-for-profit organizations, are all woven together into the social fabric of American and many other societies.

4. The same human beings function in both "religious" and "secular" organizations and spaces.

5. There is no religiously or ideologically neutral philosophy, social science, or political system.

Based on these five affirmations of some of my basic presuppositions and considered judgments,[1] we may ask, which system(s) of public, territorial governance can do the greatest justice (an admittedly non-neutral aim) to (1) religiously and ideologically diverse ways of life, (2) to the full gamut of social organizations and institutions (whether self-identified as religious or secular), and (3) to every person, of whatever faith, who exercises responsibility in any or all of those organizations and institutions?

If I read him correctly, Berger believes that the failure of secularization theory is due to its empirically inadequate and potentially prejudiced judgment that modernization leads to the end of religions, or at least to their marginalization in social discourse. He also believes that religion and secularity need not be in conflict. Furthermore, he believes that the expansion of secular space can continue progressively and peacefully—with no negative impact on religious vitality—if religions agree to distinguish between their ultimate and penultimate concerns and agree to treat only their ultimate or core beliefs as non-negotiable. Berger believes that this approach recognizes the fact of continuing religious vitality, and that it will relegate secularization theory to the dustbin. I take it that the kind of pluralism he defends theologically is what he hopes all religions will adopt,

---

1. The full framework supporting these affirmations as well as the argument that follows is developed in my book, Skillen, *Good of Politics*, 117–95.

so they can learn to live side by side in the same societies and negotiate cooperatively to shape civic peace in a religiously neutral way.

I agree with Berger that if we want to live in civic peace with our neighbors, then all, or a large majority of citizens will need to support the kind of civic order that disallows any religious or ideological way of life to impose its views on everyone by law. To understand how this is possible I believe we must be cognizant of a wide range of empirical questions and normative judgments about how certain parts of the world arrived at limited governments, under the rule of law, that gradually eliminated government control over religious authority, or vice versa. Yet such an understanding depends on recognition of the conflicts among different normative views of life, society, government, and religion. Those conflicts forced, and continue to force, constitutional, legislative, and judicial decisions about the constitution of political order.

This is not the place to try to analyze some of the conflicts in the United States that have arisen from religiously deep sources, including conflicts over the treatment of Native Americans, over slavery leading to the Civil War and subsequent degradation of African Americans, over WASP mistreatment of Catholics, and over political corruption, public/private schooling, educational curricula, civil rights for all citizens, abortion, same-sex marriage, and more. But simply listing these makes the point that religions and religiously equivalent ideologies amount to more than ways of worship (or non-worship) and professions of core beliefs. All of them play out in ways of life that may be either pure or highly synthetic, either conflict-oriented or accommodative. And therefore, any adequate theory of pluralism must deal with social-institutional diversity as well as with confessional diversity in order to assess the vitality, interchanges, and conflicts of contemporary religions and religiously equivalent ideologies.

As a social theorist, Peter Berger is concerned primarily with finding an empirically adequate replacement for the failed secularization theory. As a Christian, he wants to reflect theologically in a way that supports the kind of pluralism that promotes the coexistence of people of diverse faiths in the same societies. As a Christian social and political theorist, I join Berger in wanting to develop a theory of pluralism adequate to displace secularization theory. And as a Christian citizen, I want to support the kind of constitutional political order that upholds justice for all citizens regardless of their non-negotiable core beliefs. But I also want a political order that guarantees the equitable treatment of all citizens in their diverse religious and ideological *ways of life* as they attend to the education of their children and the conduct of their vocations, employment, personal relationships, and civic responsibilities. The kind of constitutional political system that can do this, in my estimation, is principled pluralism, by which I mean a political system in which government is obligated to uphold pluralism as a matter of principle, including both *structural pluralism* and *confessional pluralism*.

Structural Pluralism

No one can avoid making normative judgments about their lives and the kind of society in which they want to live. In recognition of that human condition, I want to contend for the kind of political system that constitutionalizes limited government, and publicly and legally recognizes and protects non-government institutions and organizations as well as individual rights such as free speech, freedom of association, and religious freedom. That kind of political/social system has not been built, and cannot be built, on religiously and philosophically neutral presuppositions. Nor can any other idea of a normative political and social system be built on a religiously and philosophically neutral basis.

A limited-government, rule-of-law, equal-treatment system can and should be defended on a Christian basis. More than that, I think such a system finds its deepest normative roots in biblical presuppositions. Jews and Christians have for millennia confessed that God is the creator of all things, including humans created in the image of God, and that humans bear a wide range of creation-wide responsibilities before God. That is the basis for the judgment that government should recognize and protect the dignity of every person and do justice to all human responsibilities, most of which are not civic or governmental (thus, *structural* pluralism). From this point of view, one reason that governments ought to be constitutionally delimited and bound by the rule of law is that humans are more than political creatures; they are also farmers and artisans, children and parents, worshippers and thinkers, engineers and artists, all of which are expressions of the image of God. A just public order certainly needs to uphold the common public good for all citizens, and in order for there to be justice for all, there must be public-legal protection of that wide diversity of non-political responsibilities.

Upholding structural pluralism as a matter of principle should be constitutionally stipulated as a mandatory responsibility of democratic government. This means that government may not overstep its authority by trying to exercise responsibilities outside its jurisdiction. It also means that within its own public-legal jurisdiction, government must assure the non-prejudicial treatment of all its citizens on a fair and equitable basis. Part of the meaning of limited government, in this sense, is that neither the constitution of a polity nor its government should have the ultimate authority to decide how humans should relate to God. Human identity and responsibility come from the Creator, not from a government or political constitution. Many citizens may choose to understand their lives as non-religious, or as divided between religious and secular domains, or as comprehensively religious. But in their civic capacity and in the diversity of their other organizational and institutional responsibilities, humans should be recognized as having the responsibility to think and act in keeping with their way of life within the bounds of a civic order of public justice.

Confessional Pluralism

Confessional pluralism is the second dimension of the public-legal principle I'm advocating. Its grounds are *not* the diversity of responsibilities humans exercise by virtue of their created nature, but rather the fact that people respond differently to God. From a biblical point of view, love and service rendered to the true God is the only proper response that accords with human identity and responsibility. All other responses, ranging from the denial that God exists to the worship of false gods, are idolatry. But the Bible is also clear that as of today God continues to mercifully uphold the entire creation, including idolaters, skeptics, atheists, and the faithful until the final judgment that God alone will execute. The Gospel of Matthew presents Jesus saying that God's rain and sunshine now fall on the just and the unjust alike (Matt 5:45) and that his followers are not authorized to compel the separation of believers from unbelievers in this world (Matt 13:24-30, 36-43). One implication of these passages (and they do not stand alone) is the principle of confessional pluralism—equal treatment under public law for all people regardless of their faithful or faithless response to God. God's merciful patience does not affirm or imply that atheism, idolatry, and true faith are equally good, but it requires of Christians the kind of merciful, equitable treatment of their neighbors that is expressive of God's patience and mercy toward all people. Since God is the source of rain and sunshine for all, and since Jesus' followers have been given no responsibility to execute final judgment, obedience to God entails the obligation to do justice equitably to all neighbors.

If we join confessional pluralism to structural pluralism as a matter of public-legal principle, and if we recognize that no aspect or responsibility of human life is religiously or ideologically neutral, then it is unjust to constitute a political system or establish a legal statute that defines society (or any part of society) as independent of God or religiously neutral. As a matter of public law it is perfectly legitimate to identify social diversity, that is, to distinguish churches from universities, families from business enterprises, and profit-making corporations from nonprofit organizations in order to do right by each of them. However, if public law attaches the word *religion* exclusively to church life, verbal expressions of faith, and self-defined "religious" nonprofits and thereby marginalizes them from the "secular" commons, the implication is that everything outside that narrow religious domain is secular in the modern sense of the term. Such an understanding of religion and the secular is itself grounded in a religiously equivalent, non-neutral, dualistic view of the whole of life.

I propose principled pluralism as an alternative paradigm. From the standpoint of principled pluralism, the public-legal enforcement of laws grounded in a dualistic view of life will mean the unjust treatment of citizens. If, instead, all citizens are recognized as having the same civil rights and protections under the law, including freedom to practice their religions, then public-legal impartiality and non-discriminatory treatment of all religions and ideological views of life are upheld as a matter of constitutional principle.

Again, I want to emphasize that what I've just proposed does not stand on religiously neutral ground; it is not free of religious presuppositions. Yet fundamental to it is the principle that government has no authority to compel any citizen to profess a particular belief, including belief in the philosophy behind what I've proposed or belief in the religious faith of those who support it. What government may compel is that people comply nonviolently with existing laws, while being free to work, on the basis of their deepest convictions, for changes through the democratic process that is open to all on a nondiscriminatory basis. This is the point at which my agreement and disagreement with Berger can be clarified. Insofar as he believes that a church institution or the core belief of a particular religion or ideology should not have a constitutional monopoly of the political system that would allow it to impose its view of life on all citizens, I am in full agreement with him. Yet insofar as he believes that "secular" responsibilities across the board are religiously neutral, or without religious presuppositions, and that a political system should be constituted to allow a so-called "secular" way of life to marginalize so-called "religious" ways of life by means of public discrimination against them, then I clearly disagree.

Public Funding of Education

Let me illustrate this difference with an example. In nineteenth-century America, the politically dominant WASP majority reacted negatively to large-scale immigration of Roman Catholics in the 1840s by calling on cities and then states to control tax-collected funding of schools for the advantage of WASP schooling.[2] Their decisions, beginning in New York City and Boston, included laws stipulating the kind of schools that would be eligible to receive public funding. Eligible schools—"common schools"— would have to be non-sectarian, in contrast to "sectarian" (chiefly Catholic) schools. The fact was that the so-called non-sectarian schools were not religiously neutral; they were thoroughly Protestant or Protestant-deist in character, with prayers, readings from the King James Bible, and moral instruction that promoted the WASP worldview. Although publicly organized and funded common schools were not religious in the sense of being run by churches or affiliated with them, they were clearly religious in expressing the civil-religious moralism of the WASP majority at the time. One ideology was privileged by public law to the disadvantage of others: the common schools received government funding, but other schools did not. The laws governing education specifically indicated that the reason for excluding Catholic schools from funding was their "sectarian" nature. Cities and states were thus deciding what was acceptable religion and what was unacceptable religion in the education of the republic's citizens. There was no "secular" space there.

The structure of that system of education funding still exists in the United States today and has continually created conflict, controversy, and numerous Supreme Court decisions. Until about the 1940s a WASP civil

---

2. The discussion on the American system of schooling that follows here depends on many sources. See Glenn, *Ambiguous Embrace*; Glenn, *Myth*; McCarthy and Skillen et al., *Disestablishment*.

religion dominated instruction in the government-run schools. Among other things, that instruction conveyed a view of life that related the nation as a whole to America's god. Although promotion of the American Way of Life was conducted primarily through the common schools, not in churches, most Protestant churches and families found themselves in agreement with it. Those who held a different view of the way schooling should be related to public life—Catholics in particular—were simply relegated by law to second-class status when it came to the funding and legal recognition of their schools. Catholics and other "sectarians" had to pay for their schools with private funds while also being required to pay taxes to support the so-called nonsectarian schools.

With the passing of years, a continuing secularization of public consciousness led to a series of U.S. Supreme Court decisions that mandated the removal of Bible reading and prayers from the common, public schools. A prejudicial belief in the secular neutrality of non-sectarianism pushed its adherents to demand the elimination of anything that looked like sectarianism in the schools, which now was perceived to include much of the WASP teaching that once was the standard of non-sectarianism. Yet the judgment of what was sectarian and nonsectarian remained in the hands of governments and the courts. Nothing changed in the structure of discriminatory funding, which has continued to flow to so-called non-sectarian public schools and sometimes to certain "non-sectarian" aspects of independent religious schools. The combination of the words *nonsectarian*, *public*, *secular*, and *common* continues to provide cover for the belief that government-funded schooling is not religious, despite the secularized, civil-religious ideology that infuses its curricula and its rules for teachers. So-called sectarian schools are still allowed to exist under the law and in most states are recognized as performing an approved educational function. But such schools (or the students who attend them) are not eligible on an equitable basis for public funding.

A genuinely pluralist system of governance would operate in a different way with respect to schooling. First, government would recognize that its public-legal responsibility includes matters such as assuring that all children receive an equitably funded education regardless of their religious affiliation or choice of school. At the same time, government would recognize that school-aged citizens are "not mere creatures of the state."[3] They are also children in families, and students in schools. Doing justice to all three of these institutions—political community, family, and school—would mean that the principle of structural pluralism requires government to distinguish its responsibility from the responsibilities of families and schools. For government to overlook or treat unfairly the responsibilities of families and schools would be to do injustice to the very citizens who are supposed to receive equal treatment under the law. If there is public funding for schooling and if all children are required by law to receive an education, then public funding should go to all children (or to their families or to the schools they attend) on the same impartial and all-inclusive basis.

The principle of confessional pluralism would require that government treat all families and schools without favor toward, or prejudice against, their religious and ideological differences. In that view, the constitution and government of the political community—the American republic in this case—has no authority to pre-define the nature of religion or to privilege one religious or ideological view of life over others. If parents (with their inherent familial responsibilities) choose to send their children to a government-run school, a Catholic school, a socialist school, or an independent school with some other religious or ideological worldview, that choice would be inconsequential with regard to government's equitable treatment of all school-eligible citizens. Likewise, any school or home schooling arrangement approved under the law should not suffer discrimination from government with respect to the funding of its students.

Conclusion

It seems to me that Berger recognizes the need for equal treatment of religious diversity by government with regard to church-type institutions and private professions of faith. However, since Berger believes we should consider secular spaces to be without religious presuppositions, he would probably accept the current system that distinguishes "sectarian" from "nonsectarian" schools and funds only the latter. If I am correct about

---

3. From U.S. Supreme Court decision *Pierce v. Society of Sisters*, 268 U.S. 510 (1925), which struck down an Oregon law that required all children to attend public schools. Despite the Court's ruling that upheld the right of parents to choose independent schools, it did not rule against the inequitable system of funding that privileged government-run schools.

this, then Berger's desire to displace secularization theory with a pluralist theory goes only as far as recognizing the empirical fact that many traditional religions continue to exist and even flourish. His pluralist theory is not sufficient, however, to assess the vitality and just treatment of religions that operate beyond the narrow boundaries of "religion" as he defines it. Nor does his theory begin to come to grips with the reality of religiously equivalent ideologies and philosophies that have gained majoritarian influence in the United States and elsewhere to shape the structure and functions of government and other institutions in ways that do not uphold equitable pluralism. Only by giving attention to the reach and influence of all religions and ideologies and by dealing with the actual identity and role of constitutional government will it be possible, as I see it, for Berger to develop a full-blown replacement for secularization theory. I, for one, want him to succeed in doing that.

Bibliography

Berger, Peter L. *The Many Altars of Modernity: Toward a Paradigm for Religion in a Pluralist Age*. Boston: De Gruyter, 2014.

Glenn, Charles L. *The Ambiguous Embrace: Government and Faith-Based Schools and Social Agencies*. Princeton, NJ: Princeton University Press, 2000.

———. *The Myth of the Common School*. Amherst, MA: University of Massachusetts Press, 1988.

McCarthy, Rockne M., et al. *Disestablishment a Second Time: Genuine Pluralism for American Schools*. Grand Rapids: Eerdmans, 1982.

Skillen, James. *The Good of Politics: A Biblical, Historical, and Contemporary Introduction*. Grand Rapids: Baker Academic, 2014.

U.S. Supreme Court. *Pierce v. Society of Sisters*, 268 U.S. 510, 1925.

6

Hindu Nationalism against Religious Pluralism—or, the Sacralization of Religious Identity and Its Discontents in Present-Day India

by Thomas A. Howard

Professor of History and the Humanities
Phyllis and Richard Duesenberg Chair in Christian Ethics
Valparaiso University
Valparaiso, Indiana

Peter Berger made news—at least in academic circles—two decades ago when he announced that "secularization theory" or the "secularization thesis" was "essentially mistaken." This thesis, long cherished by social scientists, asserted that modernity necessarily led to the withdrawal of religion from both individual and public consciousness. Berger concluded that the empirical evidence simply did not support the thesis; societies in the late modern world—with the exception of those in Western Europe, perhaps—evinced considerable religious vitality, and scholars deluded themselves in sticking with the old paradigm. I applauded then and applaud now Berger's *volte-face*. At the same time, I felt that the term he offered in the 1990s, "desecularization," failed to capture the religious dynamics of our age.[1] Fortunately, in 2014 he published *The Many Altars of Modernity*, which provides a more nuanced understanding of religious pluralism in our globalized world.[2] This book, as he writes in the introduction, "was an exercise in sociological analysis, without any religious presupposition."

1. See Berger, *Desecularization*. Cf. Berger, "Secularism in Retreat," 3–13.
2. Berger, *Many Altars*, 3, 10.

Hindu Nationalism against Religious Pluralism

No book can be expected to do all things; *Many Altars* was no exception. Some Christians and other readers with a religious bent understandably asked if our pluralistic age is good or bad for religion, and, further, how exactly believers are supposed to comport themselves in this setting. We are grateful—speaking theologically as well as sociologically—to Berger for taking up these questions in the introduction to this volume. Here, he asserts that, if encountered with the right disposition, a pluralistic setting is on balance a good thing for people of faith, whether Christian or otherwise. Pluralism, he elaborates, can provide new insights into one's faith and new insights about the purpose of religious community—for Christians, the church. It can also help believers distinguish "the core of the faith from its more peripheral aspects." These observations seem on the mark.

Berger says relatively little, however, about what happens to religious groups that reject pluralism and/or encounter it with a misguided disposition. He simply labels them "fundamentalist." He defines this fraught term as an assertion of faith "based on allegedly certain beliefs [that bestow] an allegedly certain identity. It is fierce in repelling or repressing any criticisms. It is almost impossible to reason with it."

This response takes its cue from these lines. What happens, I ask in what follows, when an influential religious community regards pluralism as a danger, and attempts to overcome it or thwart it? My engagement with the question will take the form of an extended reflection on a travel experience in India—a cauldron of religious pluralism—that took place in the summer of 2016. More concretely, I offer an overview on how a certain expression of religious fundamentalism there, "Hindutva" (Hindu nationalism), has sought in recent decades to move Indian society away from "choice" and back to "fate"—to use Berger's terms (i.e., to work against the freedom of conscience in India's Constitution by sacralizing and spreading a specific notion of Hindu identity). This effort cannot be interpreted simply as a retreat into the past, even though, as we shall see, Hindu nationalists are quite preoccupied with India's past. Rather, it represents a marriage of certain aspects of traditional Hindu identity with a European import: nationalism. Whether fundamentalism is the precise term for it, I am not sure, but the net result is a curious blend of religious nostalgia, on the one hand, and a modernizing, homogenizing political force, on the other. Many Indians resonate with this—some quite strongly. But religious minorities in India, especially Muslim and Christian communities, have good reason to regard it as a threat to religious pluralism in India and the constitutional freedoms that safeguard it.

Hindutva among the Gods

After traveling in the United States, G. K. Chesterton famously described America as "a nation with the soul of a church." Something akin to this could be said of India, but to church one must quickly add Buddhist *stupa*, Jain *mandir*, Sikh *gurdwara*, Parsi *dar-e mihr*, Muslim mosque, and, not least, Hindu temple. Indeed, the turbulently modernizing nation bristles with religious energy and diversity; it's an entire subcontinent providing evidence supportive of Berger's *volte-face*. Anyone wedded to the tired notion that modernity leads necessarily to secularization would do well to visit this seventy-year-old republic.

But secularization should not be confused with secularism. The former, again, bespeaks the withdrawal of religious sentiment from social institutions and individual consciousness. The latter is a constitutional arrangement that seeks to safeguard religious freedom and practice, and one, as Berger rightly notes, that more often produces pluralism than irreligion.[3] The Indian Constitution (1950), which echoes the U.S. model, gives expression to secularism in this sense, stating in Article 25 that "all persons are equally entitled to freedom of conscience and the right freely to profess, practice, and propagate religion."

But as I learned while in India, the reality gainsays the blueprint, and today there is reason for disquiet due to the rising menace of Hindu nationalism and its ideology of religious communalism—about which, more later. Our study team—comprising ten American scholars and ten Indian scholars, journalists, and activists supported by the Nagel Institute for the Study of World Christianity at Calvin College—traveled to the cities of Bangalore, Chennai, and Delhi. Our remit: to understand issues pertaining to religious freedom in India today and to think about the relationship of religion to social and economic development.

The ideology of Hindutva (literally, "Hindu-ness") is encouraged and transmitted by the ruling Bharatiya Janata Party (BJP, Indian People's Party). It poses a threat to the secular consensus that goes back to the post-1947 founding era, and the leadership of Gandhi and Jawaharlal Nehru, India's first Prime Minister. Under BJP rule, persecution of religious minorities,

---

3. For further reflections on this distinction, see Asad, *Formations*, 1–17.

especially Muslims and Christians, has markedly increased. The many Christian leaders in the country with whom we spoke, almost to a person, voiced grave concern about the future. In addition to worrying about their own flocks, they expressed anxiety that the West, smitten with the BJP's growth-oriented economic agenda and more preoccupied with the threat of global Islamic extremism, is blind to the constriction of religious freedom and human rights taking place in India today.

The BJP returned to power in 2014,[4] but its ideological roots go back over a century. These roots found initial expression in the late nineteenth and early twentieth century among Brahmin intellectuals disillusioned with British rule and seeking a more traditionalist basis for political and cultural identity.[5] But the proposed solution, Hindutva, should not be mistaken for Hinduism. The latter is a bewilderingly complex set of beliefs, practices, and rituals that have existed on the Indian sub-continent since time immemorial.[6] By contrast, Hindutva is a distinctly modern phenomenon, a South Asian species of what Benedict Anderson famously described as an "imagined community" (i.e., nationalism).[7] Its emergence during the late colonial period was a self-consciously homogenizing and quasi-racialist conception of Hinduism. For a Western analogue, one might point to the various religiously tinged cultural nationalisms that arose in the wake of the French Revolution and the European Romantic movement. The Protestant, fiercely anti-immigrant, nativist movement in nineteenth-century America might be another point of comparison.[8]

While many nineteenth-century figures and strands of thought could be singled out as harbingers of Hindutva, priority of place might well go to Swami Vivekananda (1863–1902). Mentioned briefly by Berger in the introduction, Vivekananda is a towering figure in modern Indian intellectual and religious history. An indefatigable international traveler who famously appeared at the Parliament of World Religions in Chicago in 1893, he sought to distill Hinduism into an essence of universal brotherly love; it was *the* primal, uncreated religion and one with the capacities to recognize and absorb the best aspects of all other world religions. What

---

4. The BJP first came to power most seriously in 1998 with Vajpayee as Prime Minister, and lost power in the 2004 elections. Stein, *History of India*.
5. Ferguson, *Empire*, 218.
6. Sen, *Hinduism*.
7. Anderson, *Imagined Communities*.
8. On American Protestant nativism, see Billington, *Protestant Crusade*.

is more, Hinduism, in his view, was the anchor of Eastern civilization, the abiding spirituality which he contrasted strongly against the materialism and individualism of Western societies.⁹ To be sure, Vivekananda's influence cuts in many directions, many peaceful and constructive. But his efforts to overcome the numerous internal differences within Hinduism and present it as one civilizational force or essence was something picked up on by later apostles of Hindutva, even if they would channel it in a more narrowly nationalist direction.¹⁰

Hindutva gained its first major public voice in Vinayak Damodar Savarkar (1883–1966), who in 1923 published *Hindutva: Who is a Hindu?* Ironically, Savarkar, who coined the term "Hindutva," was an atheist and rationalist. Self-schooled in the history of European nationalism—especially that championed by the Italian Giuseppe Mazzini—Savarkar sought to give expression to a broad cultural ideology that could challenge the British Raj, counter Western influence more generally, and provide intellectual defenses against Muslim beliefs and the allegedly culture-destroying work of Christian missionaries.¹¹ For him Indian identity, or Hindutva, was a sacred trust and cultural patrimony, but one that necessarily manifests itself in racial ("common blood") and geographical ("sacred land") terms. In his own words:

> A Hindu then is he who feels attachment to that land that extends from Sindhu to Sindhu as the land of his forefathers—as his Fatherland; who inherits the blood of the great race whose first and discernable source could be traced from the Himalayan altitudes of the Vedic Saptasindhus and which assimilating all that was incorporated and ennobling all that was assimilated has grown into and come to be known as the Hindu people; and who, as a consequence of the foregoing attributes, has inherited and claims as his own the Hindu Sanskriti, the Hindu civilization, as represented in a common history, common art, a common law and a common jurisprudence, common fairs and festivals, rites and rituals, ceremonies and sacraments.¹²

---

9. For Vivekananda's speech, see Seager, *Dawn of Religious Pluralism*, 421–32. Vivekananda was a disciple of the influential guru Ramakrishna (1836–86). On Vivekananda's debt to Ramakrishna and on Vivekananda's influence in the West after the 1893 Parliament, see Seager, *World's Parliament*, 108–71.

10. Shorma, *Restatement of Religion*.

11. On the indebtedness of Hindu nationalism to European models of the same phenomenon, see Delfs, *Hindu-Nationalismus*.

12. Savarkar, *Hindutva*, 100.

In Savarkar's view, Hindutva possessed considerable assimilative power, but there were limits to what it could absorb. He regarded Islam and Christianity in particular as foreign elements, which, while present on the Indian subcontinent, owed their deepest loyalties elsewhere and therefore could not properly be reconciled with Hindu civilization. As he bluntly put it: "Christian and Mohammedan communities, who were but very recently Hindus and in a majority of cases has [sic] been at least in their first generation most unwilling denizens of their new fold . . . *cannot be recognized as Hindus*."[13]

Within just a few years, the Hindu nationalism that Savarkar espoused took institutional form in the Rashtriya Swayamsevak Sangh (National Volunteer Society), commonly known as the RSS. Founded in 1925 by K. B. Hedgewar and consolidated later by M. S. Golwalkar, the RSS has assiduously sought to promote and protect Hindu interests and forge a "national consciousness" on the basis of Hindutva. Its mission has been remarkably consistent over the decades and today is described on the RSS website as follows:

> For the welfare of entire mankind, Bharath [India] must stand before the world as a self-confident, resurgent and mighty nation. The Rashtriya Swayamsevak Sangh has resolved to fulfill this age-old national mission by forging the present-day scattered Hindu Society into an organized and invincible force. . . . Verily this is the one real practical world mission—if ever there was one.
>
> The mission of reorganizing the Hindu society on the lines of its unique national genius that the Sangh has taken up is not only a great process of true national regeneration of Bharat but also the inevitable precondition to realize the dream of world unity and human welfare. Our one supreme goal is to bring to life the all-round glory and greatness of our Hindu Rashtra.
>
> In order to take our nation to the pinnacle of glory, the first and foremost prerequisite is the invincible organized life of the people without which even the highest national prosperity will crumble to dust in no time.
>
> Expressed in the simplest terms, the ideal . . . is to carry the nation to the pinnacle of glory through organizing the entire society and ensuring the protection of Hindu Dharma.[14]

13. Ibid.
14. RSS, "Mission."

Resembling at once a social service organization, a paramilitary operation, and a religious order, the RSS is the dominant member in a network of like-minded organizations collectively known as the "Sangh Parivar." This family of Hindu nationalist organizations also includes a workers' union, a student and youth union, a farmers' organization, and a World Hindu Council (Vishva Hindu Parishad or VHP).[15] The RSS's main ritual and recruiting mechanism has been the daily exercise or drill, known as Sangh Shakha, designed to promote bodily and mental well-being and inculcate devotion to all things Hindu.[16] Members must wear khaki shorts and show their devotion to the RSS's saffron flag. ("Saffronization" has become short-hand in India today to refer to the spread and influence of Hindu nationalism.)

The RSS grew rapidly between the 1920s and 1940s.[17] On the eve of national independence, the RSS held up a vision of nationhood that contrasted strongly with the secular, inclusivist vision put forth by Gandhi and Nehru. "The RSS," to quote the historians Barbara and Thomas Metcalf, "by contrast, put forth a vision of India as a land of, and for, Hindus. Proponents of a mystical nationalism, with racial overtones that evoked sympathetic parallels with German fascism, the RSS was stridently anti-Muslim."[18]

As is well known, Gandhi's assassination on January 30, 1948, was carried out by Nathuram Godse, a disciple of Savarkar with thick connections to the RSS. Following this traumatic event, which coincided with the bloody partition of India and Pakistan, Hindu nationalism, not surprisingly, fell into public disfavor and declined.[19] The RSS was even outlawed for a period. But its story from then until the present has been that of a steady, stealthy comeback, culminating in the landslide election of May 2014, which brought Narendra Modi (a former RSS higher-up) and the BJP party to power with large majorities in India's powerful Lok Sabha (lower parliament) and in many state assemblies.[20]

---

15. See Jaffrelot, *Sangh Parivar*.

16. On this and other practices and recruitment strategies, see Reddy, "Hindutva as Practice," 412–26.

17. Nussbaum, *Clash Within*, 155–64.

18. Metcalf and Metcalf, *Concise History*, 229.

19. Ibid., 227–35.

20. On the background and implications of this election, see Lance Prince, *Modi Effect*.

Today, the BJP functions as the political arm of the Sangh Parivar. Its comeback began in the 1980s, after it distinguished itself from other nationalist parties and developed a moderate public face. It adopted its current name in 1980, distinguishing itself from its previous identity as the Bharatiya Jana Sangh. Pledging itself to Hindutva as its official ideology, the BJP expanded its electoral footprint in the 1980s and 1990s. In 1998, for the first time, it gained more seats in parliament than Nehru's venerable India National Congress and took the prime ministership under Vajpayee. During its recent ascendancy, the BJP has maintained a tight relationship with the RSS, even if the former has often had to distance itself from the latter to broaden its public acceptance.

While it sometimes manifests itself chauvinistically, especially in its xenophobic attitude toward others who don't belong to the "homeland," Hindutva cannot be dismissed as an unsophisticated ideology. It can make a broad appeal and has survived several court cases—most notably a major one in 1995—brought about by those who felt its allure was primarily religious in nature and hence violated India's Constitution, which prohibits candidates from appealing to voters *exclusively* on religious grounds. Hindutva's defenders made the savvy counterargument that its ideology, though reflective of Hindu belief and practice, was in fact broadly "cultural" or "civilizational," not a religious movement per se, and should be viewed alongside other ideologies such as socialism or communism. As one Hindu nationalist put it, echoing the 1995 court case, Hindutva is "indicative more of a way of life of the Indian people and is not confined merely to describe persons practicing the Hindu religion as faith." Or, as the BJP's website puts it: "Hindutva is a nationalist, and not a religious or theocratic, concept."[21]

But while they attempt to cast a broad net, devotees of Hindutva share a worldview shaped by a deep sense of historical grievance. This is directed primarily at India's approximately 180 million Muslims, but also at other "foreign" religious minorities, not least Christians. In recent years, the BJP and RSS have been successful in stoking outrage at certain provisions in India's Constitution that seek to empower minorities. Special provisions in Article 370 of the Constitution for the Muslim majority in Jammu and Kashmir is one such issue. Another set of provisions, known as "reservations," ensures places for Dalits ("untouchables") and Adivasi ("tribal peoples") in universities and government bureaucracies—quotas that are widely unpopular among middle-class Brahmins, who feel shut out of

---

21. BJP, "Philosophy," lines 2–3.

positions for which they think they are better qualified. Calling for absolute uniformity in the civil code, RSS/BJP members want to end any different treatment for Muslims and other minorities. Such positions are popular not only in India, but among the wealthy Indian diaspora in the U.S., the U.K., and elsewhere, which is largely Hindu and upper-caste in its make-up and has been a key source of political and financial support back home for Hindu nationalist causes.[22]

A deep sense of grievance and injustice—with particular ire directed against the legacy of the *Muslim* Mughal Empire (ca. 1526–1857)—pervades Hindutva rhetoric and its conception of India's past.[23] A propaganda pamphlet that I acquired at the BJP headquarters' bookstore in New Delhi makes clear that "the barbaric methods of destruction of [Hindu] temples and converting Hindus to Islam [are] facts of history. . . . [I]f temples were proved to have been destroyed for construction of the mosques then they would agree that the mosque could be removed and the temple should be re-built to redress the injustice." The same pamphlet voices a widespread worry among Hindu nationalists that in India "the population of Muslims and Christians is increasing disproportionately compared to the increase in the Hindu population."[24] Although they speak of a "positive project" of cultural renewal, writes the scholar Sunil Khilnani, "in fact [Hindu nationalists] . . . are committed to a negative programme, designed to efface all signs of non-Hinduness that is . . . so integral to India."[25] Muslims, it bears mentioning, begin arriving in India not too long after the death of Mohammed; and Indian Christians, numbering today close to 30 million, trace their roots to the era of the Roman Empire and quite possibly to the missionary work of the Apostle Thomas.[26] These two religious minorities, in other words, are hardly newcomers to the subcontinent.

Intimidation and Persecution

The politics of Hindu nationalism has erupted into social intimidation and violence on numerous occasions, and it was clear to the scholars, journalists,

22. See Kurien, "Development of American Hinduism," 362–85.
23. Nussbaum, *Clash Within*, 211–63. On the Mughal Empire, see Keay, *India*, 289–413.
24. Jois, *Supreme Court*, 38.
25. Khilnani, *Idea of India*, 188–89.
26. Frykenberg, *Christianity in India*, 91–115.

and activists with whom I visited India that members of the Christian communities with whom we interacted felt more persecution was in the offing. Permit me to provide some historical context.

A major event of international notoriety occurred in 1992 when Hindu extremists—making party rhetoric reality—destroyed the historic sixteenth-century Babri mosque in Ayodhya, in the state of Uttar Pradesh. Built during the despised Mughal Empire, the mosque was believed to have been erected on the birthplace of the Hindu deity Ram. Not only was the mosque destroyed, but also the ensuing rioting in the region killed over one thousand people and poisoned the often amicable street-level relations between Muslims and Hindus. Doubling down against their critics, Hindu nationalists defended the episode as a necessary turning point in reclaiming their cultural legacy. As the Hindu activist Sadhvi Rithambhra put it: "As far as the construction of the Ram temple is concerned, some people say Hindus should not fight over a structure of brick and stone. . . . [But] it is a question of national integrity. The Hindu is not fighting for a temple of brick and stone. He is fighting for the preservation of a civilization of his Indianness, for national consciousness, for the recognition of his true nature."[27]

The reputation of the BJP suffered once more after the horrific 2002 riots in the northwestern state of Gujarat (where the governor was Narendra Modi, who later became India's prime minister). A railway carriage fire in the town of Godhra, which killed a number of Hindu pilgrims, erupted into a weeks-long, concerted massacre directed against Muslims throughout the state. For the most part, the police stood idly by as Hindu mobs, goaded by RSS activists and using government print-outs to identify minority homes, went door to door, killing, raping, and committing arson. In several documented cases, women were gang-raped and set on fire afterwards. At least 1500 Muslims died, and 150,000 took refuge in relief camps. The BJP in Gujarat paid a scant price for its complicity in these events, and when the state went to the polls in December of 2002, the BJP won re-election by large margins. For his own involvement, Modi was banned from travel to the United States—a ban awkwardly lifted once he became Prime Minister in 2014. Recrimination over the events in Gujarat persists as a regular feature of Indian politics today.

In 2008 in Orissa, a month-long spate of violence broke out against Christians after they were blamed for the death of a ninety-year-old Hindu

---

27. Khilnani, *Idea of India*, 187.

sage, Swami Lakshmanananda, and five of his companions, who in fact were likely slain by Maoist insurgents. An estimated 120 Christians, most of whom were Dalits or tribal peoples, were killed and one hundred thousand were rendered homeless. Three hundred churches and six thousand Christian homes were burned. The spotlight that these events put on Orissa led to international condemnation; on August 28, 2008, then-Pope Benedict XVI spoke for many in a speech: "I have learned with deep sadness the news about the violence against the Christian communities in the Indian State of Orissa. . . . I ask the religious leaders and civil authorities to work together to restore among the members of the various communities the peaceful coexistence and harmony which have always been the distinguishing mark of the Indian society."[28]

The Babri mosque affair, the Gujarat riots, and murders in Orissa are but three well-documented cases of Hindu-nationalist violence directed against Muslims and Christians. Violence against Christians has spiked with the political ascendancy of the BJP in recent years. Although precise figures are elusive and probably higher than reports indicate, organizations that monitor persecution in India such as Open Doors, the Catholic Bishops' Conference of India, the All India Catholic Union, the Evangelical Fellowship of India, and the recently-founded United Christian Forum for Human Rights testify to the general trend. In a 2010 communiqué, Open Doors reported that "Christians in India faced a spike of attacks in the past decade, suffering more than 130 assaults a year since 2001, with figures far surpassing that in 2007 and 2008."[29] In April of 2014, a leading human rights activist in India, my travel companion John Dayal, testified before the U.S. Congress that 153 cases of violence against Christians took place in the twelve months before the BJP swept parliament.[30] A report on the first three hundred days of Modi's rule documented 43 deaths and 600 overall cases of persecution, 149 targeting Christians and the rest Muslims—with the exception of some directed against Jews and Parsis. Specifically Christian persecution has included the burning of churches, forced "re-conversions" to Hinduism, bomb threats, the distribution of threatening literature, burning of Bibles, several high-profile rapes of nuns, the murder of priests and other Christian workers, the desecration of the Cross and statues of the Virgin, and the destruction of properties at Christian schools, colleges, and

28. See Orissa Burning, "Pope."
29. Open Doors, "India's Christians."
30. Tom Lantos HRC, "Plight of Religious Minorities in India," 16.

cemeteries. Another travel companion, Vijayesh Lal, the gregarious new director of the Evangelical Fellowship of India, wrote to me in an e-mail: "[Increasingly] Christians are treated as outsiders and targeted because they are perceived to be outsiders, i.e., people not proclaiming India as *punyabhumi* (holy land) although many consider India their *pitribhumi* (fatherland)."

During our time in India, we visited the site of St. Sebastian's, a burned church in northeast New Delhi's Dilshad Garden district. Although the arson occurred in early December of 2014, the priest, Father Anthony Francis, was still waiting for an official police report in the summer of 2016. Talking to us near the charred apse where an altar reduced to ashes once stood, the mild-mannered priest explained to us how the fire had destroyed the entire interior of the church, with the exception of a single statue of St. Jude the Apostle—the patron saint of hopeless causes! Several eyewitnesses have testified to the smell of kerosene at the time of the incident and to its presence in puddles formed by the water that eventually put out the fire. The event elicited a letter from Delhi's Archbishop Anil Couto to Prime Minister Modi, calling for a special judicial inquiry and announcing a protest to complain about police inaction.[31] As of 2015, little had been done.

Persecution of Christians does not always manifest itself in outright violence; it also comes in subtler ways. Five Hindutva-friendly state legislatures have passed so-called "anti-conversion laws," which penalize people for converting from one faith to another or require that such decisions be registered to local authorities. While so-called "homecomings" (*ghar wapsi*) to Hinduism are rarely scrutinized, Hindus who convert to Islam or Christianity can be quickly vilified and ostracized.[32] Accordingly, the number of "secret Christians" in the country, we were repeatedly told, is hard to tell. Recently, high-ranking members of the ruling BJP party, including the party's past president and current home minister, Rajnath Singh, called for a nationwide anti-conversion law. Hindu Nationalists also talk of a nationwide ban on beef—a sacred cause to them and one intended to affect the jobs and diets of Muslims and Christians. These proposals are feverishly discussed in Hindutva circles, even if nation-wide consensus concerning them is elusive.

---

31. Perappadan, "Dilshad Garden Church Attack."

32. The term can mean both returning to Hinduism or converting to it—the idea being that Hinduism is a primal religion which should gather in all peoples. Vijajan and Gabriel, "Hindutva's Psychological Warfare," 22–24.

Yet another restriction of religious freedom comes in the form of monitoring of—or outright bans on—foreign sources of funding, the lifeblood of many church organizations and other NGOs in India. These restrictions are justified by the Foreign Contributions Regulation Act (ICNL, 2010), which seeks to root out funding deemed "detrimental to the national interest."[33] Although the BJP, not without good reason, contends that these restrictions are aimed at Muslim extremists, many Christian organizations have also been targeted—including the Vatican's charity, Caritas; Mother Teresa's Sisters of Charity; and a number of evangelical organizations. Although the Indian Constitution guarantees that religious groups may propagate their faith, Hindu nationalists claim that many Christian organizations engage in coercive proselytism—especially among the Dalit classes—in a calculated "anti-India" effort to pollute national identity. Keeping Dalits in a state of subordination and upholding the caste system (technically illegal after independence but still widely recognized) is a persistent ambition of the Hindutva's more extreme voices.

Many organizations and activists within India have called attention to these developments and others. Our traveling companion Dayal, the founding Secretary General of the All India Christian Council, summarized the sentiment of many when he noted, "In recent years, human rights and freedom of faith activists within the Christian community, and in civil society, have felt that the fundamental Constitutional right of freedom to profess, practice and propagate religion [is] circumscribed . . . [This] has to be defended to prevent a further erosion of civil liberties which could alter the basic character of Indian democracy."[34]

Similar sentiments have been expressed by institutions and individuals outside of India. The 2015 Annual Report of the U.S. Commission on International Religious Freedom, for example, noted the increase in reports of violence in India in recent years and observed that a "climate of impunity" against wrongdoers appeared to exist in a number of Indian states, "exacerbating the social and religious tensions among communities." The Report recommended that the U.S. "integrate concern for religious freedom into bilateral contacts with India . . . and encourage the strengthening of the capacity of state and central police to implement effective measures to prohibit and punish cases of religious violence."[35] More recently, John

33. ICNL, "Foreign Contribution Act," 1.
34. Dayal, "Modi Government," 53.
35. USCIRF, "Annual Report 2015," 101, 150, 153.

Allen, the *Boston Globe*'s reporter on Catholicism, has run several articles on the rise of anti-Christian violence in India. Persecution in India, writes Allen, "illustrates how religious prejudice is often bound up with ethnicity and poverty. India's Christians are disproportionately likely to be drawn from the ranks of the Dalits. . . . By some estimates sixty to seventy-five percent of the country's Christians are Dalits, making them easy targets."[36] Empirical studies strongly support the validity of such claims.[37]

To the relief of religious minorities, President Obama sought to call a spade a spade on his state visit to India in January of 2015. Expressing concern that India was "splinter[ing] along the lines of religious faith," he elaborated that "religious faiths of all types have, on occasion, been targeted by other people of faith, simply due to their heritage and their beliefs—acts of intolerance that would have shocked Gandhi, the person who helped to liberate the nation."[38] The Indian colleagues with whom we traveled stressed how grateful they were for these words, even if their effectiveness remains to be seen.

Conclusion

Predictions are difficult, as the saying goes, especially when they concern the future. It is, indeed, hard to discern the near- and long-term prospects for religious freedom and the rights of religious minorities in India. On humanitarian grounds, all people of faith and good will should be concerned. But even the hardened realist ought to care. India remains Asia's leading, if fragile, democracy and a likely economic behemoth in coming decades, with which the United States will frequently have to deal. A simmering human rights calamity and frequent religious conflict is a scenario everyone should want to avoid.[39]

Much depends on the future direction of the BJP. Although the 2014 elections that returned the party to power witnessed much divisive rhetoric, the maintenance of power in a pluralistic setting often necessitates moderation. India's southern states have exhibited considerable resistance to Hindutva rhetoric. What is more, the BJP experienced a setback in 2015

36. See Allen, "Hindu Extremists," A4.
37. Bob, "Dalit Rights," 167–93.
38. For speech video, see Zezima, "Obama Lays Out Vision."
39. On projections for India's future and U.S.-Indian relations, see helpful essays in Malhotra, *Critical Decade*.

elections in the state of Bihar. Analysts observed that the party's religious fear-mongering failed to take the spotlight off more dire needs such as sanitation, drinking water, and basic health care. If this continues to occur in other states' elections, mainstream BJP politicians might be more motivated to rein in the militant among their rank and file and do more to curb widespread police inaction at the state and city level. An intimation of better times appeared in February 2015 when shortly after Obama's visit, Modi—to the dismay of nationalist hardliners—broke a long silence and proclaimed: "My government will ensure that there is complete freedom of faith and that everyone has the undeniable right to retain or adopt the religion of his or her choice without coercion or undue influence."[40]

Although the combination of political power and the religious demographics of India—soon approaching one billion Hindus compared to some two-hundred-plus million members of religious minorities—might only embolden extremists' voices in the long run and calcify a "climate of impunity" for the foreseeable future, Indian Christians, other religious minorities, and their supporters abroad need not view their situation as a hopeless cause. Unlike many East Asian countries, India still enjoys many democratic freedoms, including freedom of the press and freedom of assembly. The religious freedom codified in its constitution shines brightly in the broader Asian political landscape. India also has a rich tradition of public argument and respect for pluralism, typified in figures such as Rabindranath Tagore and, more recently, Amartya Sen. The words of Obama and Modi, furthermore, should instill a measure of gladness. Nonetheless, cause for genuine concern exists, and the novena prayer to St. Jude doubtless speaks to many Indian Christians today: "Make use, I beseech thee, of that particular privilege accorded to thee, to bring visible and speedy help where help was almost despaired of. Come to mine assistance in this great need, that I may receive the consolation and succor of Heaven in all my necessities, tribulations, and sufferings."

The robust re-assertion of India's religious freedom and the country's historic pluralism would be welcome answer to this prayer. Happily, it would also affirm the validity of Peter Berger's sociological and theological musings about Christian faith in its sojourn among the many altars of modernity.

---

40. See WSJ Staff, "Narendra Modi's Speech."

Bibliography

Allen, John L. "Hindu Extremists' Anti-Christian Violence on Rise in India." *Boston Sunday Globe* (19 July 2015) A4.

Anderson, Benedict. *Imagined Communities: Reflections on the Origin and Spread of Nationalism*. London: Verso, 1983.

Asad, Talal. *Formations of the Secular: Christianity, Islam, Modernity*. Stanford: Stanford University Press, 2003.

Berger, Peter, ed. *The Desecularization of the World: Resurgent Religion and World Politics*. Grand Rapids: Eerdmans, 1999.

Berger, Peter. *The Many Altars of Modernity: Toward a Paradigm for Religion in a Pluralist Age*. New York: De Gruyter, 2014.

———. "Secularism in Retreat." *The National Interest* 46 (Winter 1996) 3–13.

Billington, Ray Allen. *The Protestant Crusade: A Study in American Nativism*. Chicago: Quadrangle, 1964.

Bharatiya Janata Party. "BJP Philosophy: Hindutva (Cultural Nationalism)." http://www.bjp.org/about-the-party/philosophy.

Bob, Clifford. "'Dalit Rights Are Human Rights': Caste Discrimination, International Activism, and the Construction of a New Civil Rights Issue." *Human Rights Quarterly* 29 (2007) 167–93.

Dayal, John. "Modi Government Builds Tempo for National Law Banning Conversions to Christianity." *Mainstream Weekly* 53 (April 4, 2015). http://www.mainstreamweekly.net/article5580.html.

Delfs, Tobias. *Hindu-Nationalismus und europäischer Faschismus: Vergleich, Transfer- und Beziehungsgeschichte*. Hamburg: EB Verlag, 2008.

Ferguson, Niall. *Empire: How Britain Made the Modern World*. London: Penguin, 2004.

Frykenberg, R. E. *Christianity in India: From Beginnings to the Present*. Oxford: Oxford University Press, 2008.

International Center for Not-for-Profit Law (ICNL). "Foreign Contribution (Regulation) Act, 2010." http://www.icnl.org/research/library/files/India/ForeignContribution.pdf.

Jaffrelot, Christophe, ed. *The Sangh Parivar: A Reader*. New Delhi: Oxford University Press, 2005.

Jois, M. Rama, ed. *Supreme Court Judgment on "Hindutva" A Way of Life*. 3rd ed. New Delhi: Suruchi Prakashan, 2013.

Keay, John. *India: A History*. Revised Edition. New York: Grove, 2010.

Khilnani, Sunil. *The Idea of India*. New York: Penguin, 2004.

Kurien, Prema. "Multiculturalism, Immigration, and Diasporic Nationalism: The Development of an American Hinduism." *Social Problems* 51 (2004) 362–85.

Malhotra, Rajeev, ed. *A Critical Decade: Policies for India's Development*. New Delhi: Oxford University Press, 2012.

Metcalf, Barbara D., and Thomas R. Metcalf. *A Concise History of Modern India*. 3rd ed. Cambridge: Cambridge University Press, 2012.

Nussbaum, Martha C. *The Clash Within: Democracy, Violence, and India's Future*. Cambridge, MA: Belknap Press of Harvard University Press, 2009.

Open Doors USA. "India's Christians Suffer Spike in Assaults in Past Decade," last modified December 31, 2010, https://www.opendoorsusa.org/take-action/pray/Indias-Christians-Suffer-Spike-in-Assaults-in-Past-Decade.

Orissa Burning. "Pope Condemns Violence, Appeals for Peace." Last modified August 27, 2008. http://orissaburning.blogspot.com/search?q=pope+condemns+violence.

Perappadan, Bindu Shajan. "Dilshad Garden Church Attack; Archbishop Seeks Judicial Inquiry." *The Hindu* online, last modified April 7, 2016, http://www.thehindu.com/news/cities/Delhi/archbishop-writes-to-pm-wants-judicial-inquiry/article6654061.ece.

Prince, Lance. *The Modi Effect: Inside Narendra Modi's Campaign to Transform India*. New York: Quercus, 2015.

Reddy, Deepa. "Hindutva as Practice." *Religion Compass* 5 (2011) 412–26.

Rashtriya Swayamsevak Sangh (RSS). "Mission." http://rss.org/Encyc/2015/4/7/1254694.aspx.

Savarkar, Vinayak Damodar. *Hindutva: Who is a Hindu?* 5th ed. Bombay: Veer Savarkar Prakashan, 1969.

Seager, Richard Hughes, ed. *The Dawn of Religious Pluralism: Voices from the World's Parliament of Religions, 1893*. Lasalle, IL: Open Court, 1993.

———. *The World's Parliament of Religions: The East/West Encounter, Chicago, 1983*. Bloomington: Indiana University Press, 1995.

Sen, K. M. *Hinduism*. London: Penguin, 1961.

Shorma, Jyotirmaya. *A Restatement of Religion: Swami Vivikanada and the Making of Hindu Nationalism*. New Haven: Yale University Press, 2013.

Stein, Burton. *A History of India*. Edited by David Arnold, 2nd ed. Chichester, UK: Wiley-Blackwell, 2010.

Tom Lantos Human Rights Commission. "The Plight of Religious Minorities in India: Hearing before the Tom Lantos Human Rights Commission U.S. House of Representatives (4 April 2014)." https://humanrightscommission.house.gov/events/hearings/plight-religious-minorities-india.

United States Commission on International Religious Freedom (USCIRF). "Annual Report 2015." http://www.uscirf.gov/reports-briefs/annual-report/2015-annual-report

Vijajan, P. K., and Karen Gabriel. "Hindutva's Psychological Warfare: The Insidious Agendas of Ghar Wapsi." *Economic and Political Weekly* 50 (2015) 22–24.

WSJ Staff. "Narendra Modi's Speech on Minority Religions in Full." *The Wall Street Journal* online, February 8, 2015, http://blogs.wsj.com/indiarealtime/2015/02/18/narendra-modis-speech-on-minority-religions-in-full/.

Zezima, Katie. "Obama Lays Out Sweeping Vision for US-India Relations, Emphasizes Human Rights." *The Washington Post* online, January 27, 2015, https://www.washingtonpost.com/world/obama-lays-out-sweeping-vision-for-us-india-relations-emphasizes-human-rights/2015/01/27/c8f930bc-a5f6-11e4-a7c2-03d37af98440_story.html?utm_term=.c15a810164c3.

7

Gendered Wrath:
Reflections on Anger and Forgiveness

by Ruth Groenhout

Professor of Philosophy
Distinguished Professor of Healthcare Ethics
University of North Carolina Charlotte
Charlotte, North Carolina

Peter Berger's thought-provoking discussion of Christian faith in a pluralist age raises all sorts of interesting questions and potential philosophical enquiries. In this response I would like to focus on a particular issue that arises on the borderline (for me) between philosophical reflection and personal experience. The question is this: What does it mean to live as a Christian feminist in a pluralist world where many of my fellow Christians and my sister feminists consider these two relevance structures to be incompatible? A relevance structure is the general framework of concepts, categories, and taken-for-granted values that structure a given group or community of thinkers. The relevance structures of feminism, for example, include the assumption that assigning people jobs or tasks solely on the basis of sex is always suspect, while many Christians assume it to be part of the way God intends the world to function. Given the potential for conflict, is it possible to carve out room for a relatively unified sense of personal identity that allows for the co-habitation of both commitments?

I'll begin with a story, a rather mundane one, to illustrate the sorts of conflicts that one faces living in the juncture between these two relevance structures. My pastor preached a sermon on anger, one that condemned anger and wrath for the chaos and destruction they cause. His text was the story of David, Nabal, and Abigail, and he carefully pointed out the way both David and Nabal exhibited angry reactions that were guaranteed to bring down destruction on both men and their followers. Abigail offered a Christ-like alternative, calming down one wrathful man while quietly working around her husband's foolishness. So far, so good—it was a fine sermon, and well-delivered.

The problem is, while I was listening to the sermon, I was also reflecting on my own anger at behavior described on a blog titled "What is it like being a woman in philosophy?" that details page after page of sexual harassment, biased and unjust treatment, serious belittlement, and rampant sexism. Reading these accounts, and thinking about graduate students I know and have mentored who have had to fight through the horrendous barriers for women in philosophy, I find myself really angry—seething, in fact. As a feminist, further, my anger not only seems to be aimed at the right targets, it is also an emotion commonly denied women because we are supposed to be caring, nurturing, and forgiving. My pastor's sermon certainly encourages all Christians to always model these traits, using a female model as the paradigm.

Now, I realize that the sermon was a general one, based on the combination of a proverb and a narrative exemplifying that proverb in action. Every aspect of anger can't be discussed in one sermon, nor should it be. But for individuals who live between the two worlds of Christianity and feminism, the topic of anger is a particularly fraught one. In a Christian context, discussions of anger are largely negative. Though there may be occasional mention of the fact that anger seems to have its place (Jesus was, after all, quite angry during the cleansing of the temple), the general assumption is that anger needs to be given up or set aside. Most examples of anger tend to be masculine as well, with a few exceptions. Finally, anger tends to be treated as an emotion that one person feels toward another, largely a private emotion, and one that should lead the virtuous Christian toward forgiveness and reconciliation.

Now, it must be admitted that God is portrayed as angry at times, whether in Jonathan Edward's sermon "Sinners in the hands of an angry God" or God's wrath being unleashed on the prophets of Baal in the days of Elijah. But the images of God's anger, while they may fit well with our cultural assumptions about men's anger, are a poor fit for what women experience. Cultural expectations of women simply do not include the authority to condemn others to death because they fail to conform to right doctrine or worship the wrong gods. God's anger carries with it the authority of the masculine, the kingly, and those who are assumed to be legitimately dominant. When women take on authoritative roles, they are seen as usurpers, as demanding respect that they do not deserve. The common expectation of powerful women is that they will make it clear that they do not expect the sort of obedience and reverence that men in the same position are offered unthinkingly.[1] So images of God's anger rarely serve to legitimize women's anger in religious settings; more often, they serve to undermine women's anger because women do not have the right to assume the authority that righteous anger requires.

It is significant, too, that the contemporary church has moved away from regularly invoking God's anger. Partly out of a doctrinal sense that God can't really have emotions, and partly out of a general discomfort with a Christianity focused on threats and compulsory belief, much of the Western church has moved to an emphasis on God's love and compassion. The world we live in today does not easily recognize violence and death threats as part of a loving father's natural behavioral repertoire, and this is probably a good thing. But it makes scriptural portrayals of God more problematic, since that was a standard understanding of the patriarch in the days when scripture was written.

The combination of this emphasis on love, the diminished or nonexistent description of God's wrath, and general cultural expectations that women should neither express anger nor claim the authority necessary for the right to get angry and legitimately tell others how to behave—this combination of factors makes the very notion of women's anger deeply threatening and, well, unchristian. The church is comfortable with the image of Mary bowing her head and acknowledging that she is the Lord's handmaid. Gentle Mary, meek and mild, is a stock character on countless Christmas cards. But the militant Mary who composed the Magnificat, calling for the overthrow of the powerful and a revolution that would catapult the lowly into power, has never been quite so celebrated. While her song may occasionally be referenced, it is almost never portrayed as an expression of anger or righteous wrath.

From a feminist perspective, things look quite different. Feminist thinkers have pointed out that women's legitimate claims often are dismissed on the grounds that they are simply "angry feminists," and these thinkers have worked to reclaim women's anger at injustice as a source of

---

1. See Saul, "What Is It Like?"

power. Anger is a powerful, natural human emotion, and because feminists believe that women are actually human, they accept the fact that women get angry, that anger is appropriate under many circumstances, and that it is an important source of women's power. The feminist community has also had to think through the ways that women's calls for basic rights are often derided as nothing more than selfishness. The early suffragettes were portrayed, in cartoons and in opinion pieces, as lazy and self-centered, trying to usurp men's place in society and the world. (Men's rights to women's labor was, for some reason, never portrayed as laziness.) Media portrayals of second wave feminists protesting sexual harassment in the workplace emphasized their (assumed) unattractiveness and envy of other's beauty, and never acknowledged the vicious attacks many were experiencing in the workplace. And today women's voices on blogs and in op-ed pieces are the target of vicious silencing campaigns by trolls and men's rights activists. In all of these cases, women's anger at deep injustices is not recognized as legitimate, but rather treated as trivial, childlike, selfish, and demanding. The fact remains that women's expression of anger is as likely to generate threats ranging from violent rape to dismemberment and death as it is to be seen as a legitimate concern for basic human rights.

Further, because much of the anger that feminists express is focused on deep injustices, such as the continued violence and abuse women suffer worldwide, it is the sort of anger that does not generate any easy path toward forgiveness or reconciliation. It seems rather to require socially coordinated political action and resistance. In the past, in fact, simplistic calls for forgiveness often functioned as enabling mechanisms that allowed injustice to continue, and this sometimes still occurs today. Calling for the abused to forgive their abusers is an example of this dynamic; it is easy to recognize that it perpetuates abuse.[2] Calls for forgiveness also function to pathologize anger, and to make it an emotion that one (especially female ones!) ought not experience.[3] After all, if forgiveness is necessary for mental health, and anger prevents forgiveness, then anger must be unhealthy and inappropriate. Or so we are told.

The contrasting pictures of anger I have just drawn are a bit simplistic, of course, but they indicate the ways that a reflective individual can find herself living in two worlds that seem to see women's anger in quite different ways. Examining the assumptions behind these contrasting pictures of

2. Lamb, "Forgiveness Therapy," 61–80.
3. Burstow, *Radical*.

anger—especially the background assumptions regarding social power and authority that are crucial to each picture of anger—offers us a vantage point for thinking about what is at stake in each picture.

Let's start with the way anger is generally framed in Christian circles. In keeping with the sermon mentioned earlier, anger is most commonly framed as a personal issue. Individuals are angry, and their anger is a matter for them as individuals, not as members of a particular social class. Their anger is directed toward another individual, usually because that other individual has done something harmful or insulting—something that the angry person perceives as directed at herself or himself. Moreover, the harm involved is often relatively petty—an insult to one's honor, perhaps, or a failure to fulfill a contractual obligation. The assumption, generally, is that both the angered victim and the perpetrator stand in roughly equal positions, so that the victim could, if he or she so chose, retaliate against the perpetrator. Calls to forgiveness address that capacity to retaliate. They call on the *victim* to stop the cycle of violence—to refrain from retaliation so that peace can prevail. These calls to forgiveness usually are accompanied by some sort of assurance that the victim will be healed, or will experience peace, or will become a better person overall if she or he forgives, and gives up the anger they currently feel.

In many ways this is a very important narrative for the church to offer the broader society. We all recognize the ways that one person's harm to another can trigger an endless cycle of retribution that spreads out like ripples in a pond. Further, it is true that unresolved anger, especially anger over personal harms suffered, can magnify the harms by causing the victim to relive them over and over again, each time re-inscribing the hurt, the anger, and the frustration. Learning to let go of this anger can be a crucial part of healing and peace, as Patricia Raybon details in some of her work.[4] The Christian narrative on forgiveness and its challenge to feelings of anger and resentment offers a legitimate sense of healing and wholeness under some circumstances. More than this, it offers a powerful sense of agency to those who have been wronged. In turning away from anger I refuse to allow another to hold power over my emotions. I become the one who controls what matters to me, and I no longer am held hostage to the one who caused me harm in the first place. This claiming of agency and assertion of control is a central aspect of the healing power of forgiveness and a reason to

---

4. Raybon, *First White Friend*.

recognize that in many cases, hanging on to anger can be more damaging to the one who suffers than to the one who caused the anger in the first place.

Under some circumstances, forgiveness and reconciliation can offer a far better way to move forward than the alternative of retribution. However, in some other contexts calls to forgive can function in far less positive ways. My concern here is with the phenomenon of a community calling too quickly for a victim to forgive, which implicitly expresses more concern for the community's emotional comfort than for the well-being of the victim, or the need for justice. Consider, for example, the advice offered on the website Life Coaching for Christian Women, where as an enquiring reader I discover that since all the paths of life are full of God's loving kindness, I should never allow myself to get angry. God has placed "small annoyances" in my pathway to make me grow spiritually, and if I refuse to accept them as the loving will of God, then I am the one who fails. God's "tough love" is designed to make me grow, after all![5] Perhaps the advice we find here is appropriate for small, everyday slights, but it is not appropriate at all for serious abuse, serious injustice, sexual harassment. Imagine a woman whose sexist colleagues in her college subject her to a continuous barrage of denigration and harassment. Imagine, further, that these same colleagues treat their young female students as little more than sexual prospects, available for the taking. She watches as they derail bright young women from promising careers, undermine other female colleagues, and treat women, generally, in ways that destroy the women's sense of confidence, self, or purpose. To respond in such a situation with a cheery "Well, all this is just God's tough love!" is perverse. These issues require that we stand up to them—that anger functions as a call to justice and political action. And the issue does not arise solely in the context of gender relations; for African-American women and others it can arise in racial contexts as well.

Consider, for example, the response by many white churches to the civil rights movement in the fifties and sixties. Civil rights activists were committed to nonviolence, but were being met with vicious attacks and imprisonment. Many Northern churches issued official letters calling on the civil rights workers to cease their actions, and to accept the unjust and oppressive laws and social structures they faced. Perhaps legal challenges to segregation were acceptable, but marches and sit-ins were asserted to be far too aggressive—not at all fitting for followers of Christ.[6] I hardly need to

---

5. See *Life Coaching for Christian Women*, "How to Deal with Anger."
6. Lawson, "Freedom," 456–71.

point out how misguided these claims were. Martin Luther King's "Letter from a Birmingham Jail" said all that needed to be said, though quite a lot still needed to be done. But it is not as if the Christians of that day were so very different from Christians today. The general tendency of privileged members of the Christian church to prefer a quick resolution via forgiveness, rather than the hard work of struggling for justice, remains with us today just as much as in the past.

For those who already live lives structured by privilege and power, the anger of those faced with injustice is both frightening and unnerving. If those touched by police violence against the black community insist on reminding us that black lives matter, and if women confronting deep sexism in the workplace insist that they should be treated as human beings, not convenient sexualized objects, then we have to pay attention to the structural problems that our society has generated. But it is far easier to ignore the co-worker telling sexist jokes, or the professor hitting on his graduate student, than to respond and call those who already have power to account. So the temptation, always, is to insist that those on the receiving end of violence, injustice, and oppression accept their lot in life and exercise forgiveness toward those who have power.

This dynamic seems particularly strong in the case of cultural expectations that women will forgive, an expectation shared by both men and women. Because these expectations are internalized, women often place higher expectations on themselves to forgive than men do; women participate more in practices of forgiveness, and more frequently undergo psychological therapies based on forgiveness.[7] Women, in other words, are socialized to see their own anger as dangerous and unacceptable, and to feel anxious if they fail to smooth over the situation. Rather than teaching women to protest when they experience injustice, we place on them the heavy burden of being peacemakers, even when—or precisely when—they are the ones suffering injustice. And the injustice they suffer is a structural injustice—not solely a personal insult, but unfair treatment that is targeted at them because they are women, and because women need to be put in their place. When women's place is defined as one of submission and servitude, a quick resort to forgiveness serves to perpetrate injustice, not confront it.

Further, research into how onlookers perceive and process other people's anger has established that there is a tendency for the anger of those with less social power to be dismissed, belittled, and treated as illegitimate.

---

7. Norlock, *Forgiveness*, 61–80.

In a recent study, a simulation of jury deliberation, researchers found that male jurors who were perceived as angry gained persuasive power in deliberations, while the opposite was the case for female jurors who expressed anger; not only were they dismissed, but their anger was seen as justification for holding views that contradicted theirs.[8] Women themselves internalize the expectation that anger is inappropriate and deserves punishment, and often try to suppress their feelings; researchers have found that when women are successful, and bypass awareness of their anger, they are at a higher risk for anxiety and panic attacks.[9] There are any number of books designed to teach women how to manage their anger, but far too few that address the question of how the unfair treatment that generates that anger might be alleviated.

When the anger women experience is generated by problematic experiences and structures within the church itself, it is especially disturbing to be met with calls for forgiveness without much concern to fix the conditions causing the anger. As Sharon Lamb notes in her discussion of forgiveness therapy, there are types of harms for which forgiveness appears simply wrong, particularly when what one is called to forgive is not a purely personal attack, but instead is violence or injustice directed at an individual as a member of a specific group. Hate crimes are characterized, in part, by the creation of an environment of silencing, fear, and intimidation. Quick calls for forgiveness under these circumstances can represent a betrayal of others who are also subject to these same attacks.[10] So, in the church, when women are faced with structures that prevent their full participation, they are frequently told that they need to forgive, to respond in love, and to demonstrate gentleness and meekness toward those treating them with disdain. That gentleness, unfortunately, allows the same exclusion to be exercised toward other women, and toward other people positioned in socially inferior positions.

It is tempting, then, to give free rein to one's anger. Especially when one's cause is just, and the other toward whom one's anger burns is clearly bigoted and unfair, it seems permissible—perhaps even required—that one let that anger rip! This other side of the anger coin can be found in feminist circles. In that context, women's anger is seen as legitimate, and the popular societal dismissal of women's anger is seen as one component of a system

---

8. Salerno and Peter-Hagene, "Angry Woman," 581–92.
9. Cox et al., *Women's Anger*.
10. Lamb, "Forgiveness," 45–60.

deeply biased against women. Because of the concern about how charges of being an angry feminist are used to silence women, and because of a recognition of the way those with more social power tend to dismiss the anger of victims of injustice, feminists have seen anger as both legitimate and worthy of respect. Anger is a strong emotion, a source of power, and produces resistance to a sexist status quo.[11]

At the same time, this is a context in which anger, and calls for redress against injustice, can sometimes become far too self-justifying. Soft answers do often turn aside wrath, and it is in living with sexist men over the years, and continuing to be in relation with them, that I have seen real change occur. There are a range of situations, of course, and in my experiences with colleagues who are true sexual predators, I have found that forgiveness, gentleness, and conciliation are all completely wrong. True harassers feel no guilt about what they do and consider mercy a sign of weakness. Confronted with such an individual, the right response is not forgiveness and second chances, but the full force of any legal penalties available.

But in cases of colleagues who are simply unthinking in their sexism—who intend to be decent human beings, but who have been socialized in a deeply male-dominated society, and who unthinkingly assume male privilege—it is not always the case that giving free rein to anger is the right response to everyday acts of sexism. It feels good to lash out, of course, and when one is in the right, it also feeds one's sense of moral superiority. But changing a workplace culture takes long-term relationships and continued interactions with others. Those long-term relationships require generosity of spirit, if not full-fledged forgiveness, and a willingness to see progress where insult still exists.

Recognition that one's anger is righteous is a powerful experience, and women's reclamation of the power of their anger is an important force for social change. But righteous anger easily turns into self-righteousness, a blindness to the weakness and humanity of the other, and a willingness to take revenge at any cost. Christian treatments of anger are valuable reminders in my life that those others, annoying and frustrating as they may be, are still made in the very image of God, and still deserve a level of compassion and mercy, even when what they have done is deeply problematic.

So while I often feel as though I live between two worlds when it comes to the issue of anger, in many ways this is a healthy place to live. When calls from the church to forgive become facile dismissals of deep

11. Brown, *Raising Their Voices*.

injustices that do need to be addressed, my feminist training helps me stand up and reject the silencing of "forgiveness" mandates. When a legitimate concern for justice and sensitivity slides into self-righteous attacks on folks who are simply naïve and unthinking, my Christian suspicion of anger can come in handy as a reality check. But more than giving me insight into other people's legitimacy, these two different ways of framing anger allow me to gain some perspective on my own responses. When I am angry at the normal idiocy of the everyday, my Christian colleagues are right to remind me that letting go of such anger is healthy, and part of living as a Christian in a difficult world. Though I rarely want to hear it, and though I always want to consider my anger justified, there are times when, honestly, I need to let it go.

At the same time, when those calls to let it go are coming from folks who are clearly made uncomfortable by any confrontation of structural injustices, or when I'm told to forgive by Christians who never, themselves, stand up for much of anything, my feminist suspicion of such techniques is often warranted. Calls for forgiveness, and for letting go of anger, should never be issued in the absence of public truth-telling and acceptance of institutional complicity in creating structural injustice.[12] Christians need to be aware of how their pious calls for forgiveness can reflect, and sometimes entrench, complacency in the face of injustice. Feminists would do well to recognize that not every sexist act or comment need be an occasion for attack.[12] Somewhere between these two relevance structures, in a world where pluralism provides both challenges and wisdom, is a place where both activism and gentleness become possible. And when I find that place, I'll let you know!

Bibliography

Arms, Margaret. "When Forgiveness Is Not the Issue in Forgiveness: Religious Complicity in Abuse and Privatized Forgiveness." *Journal of Religion and Abuse* 4 4 (2003) 107–28.

Brown, Lyn Mikel. *Raising Their Voices: The Politics of Girls' Anger*. Cambridge, MA: Harvard University Press, 1999.

Burstow, Bonnie. *Radical Feminist Therapy: Working in the Context of Violence*. New York: Sage, 1992.

Cox, Deborah, et al. *Women's Anger: Clinical and Developmental Perspectives*. New York: Brunner/Mazel, 1999.

12. Arms, "When Forgiveness," 107–28.

Lamb, Sharon. "Forgiveness Therapy: The Context and Conflict." *Journal of Theoretical and Philosophical Psychology* 25 (2005) 61–80.

———. "Forgiveness, Women, and Responsibility to the Group." *Journal of Human Rights* 5 (2006) 45–60.

Lawson, Steven. "Freedom Then, Freedom Now: The Historiography of the Civil Rights Movement." *The American Historical Review* 96 (1991) 456–71.

Life Coaching for Christian Women, "How to Deal with Anger." http://www.lifecoachingforchristianwomen.com/resources/self-directed-coaching/article-index/everyday-life-how-to-deal-with-anger/

Norlock, Kathryn. *Forgiveness from a Feminist Perspective*. Lanham, MD: Lexington, 2008.

Raybon, Patricia. *My First White Friend: Confessions on Race, Love, and Forgiveness*. New York: Penguin, 1997.

Salerno, Jessica M., and Lianna Peter-Hagene. "One Angry Woman: Anger Expression Increases Influence for Men, but Decreases Influence for Women, during Group Deliberation." *Law and Human Behavior* 36 (2015) 581–92.

Saul, Jenny. "What Is It Like to be a Woman in Philosophy?" https://beingawomaninphilosophy.wordpress.com/2016/06/24/what-is-it-like-to-be-a-woman-in-philosophy

8

Evangelical Christianity and Women's Roles in Contemporary Brazil: Marginalization or Modernization?

Ruth M. Melkonian-Hoover

Associate Professor of Political Science
Gordon College
Wenham, Massachusetts

Introduction

The world is becoming more religious, not less, as Peter Berger asserts; and in the developing world, more women are converting to or remaining within religions rather than becoming secularized.[1]

In Brazil, pluralist forces have helped create space for the rise of evangelical women. Post military-rule in 1988, the new Brazilian constitution dis-established the Catholic Church as the state church, protecting freedom of conscience, of belief, and of the practice of religion, making it easier for women to exercise choice in faith. Catholicism was further removed from its hegemony by its association in the public's mind with the prior military regime.

Interestingly, pluralism has been stimulated in Brazil not so much by science and technology, as Berger proposes, but by the disparate agendas of secular leftist parties that favor a strong separation of church and state, and by a multiplicity of religious actors that desire freedom of religion, both of which converge to further undermine Catholic dominance in political leadership. Given choices that were not earlier available, a significant

1. Berger, *Desecularization*.

number of women (along with men) in Brazil have converted to evangelicalism, particularly Pentecostalism: approximately one fifth of the Brazilian population is evangelical, and over two thirds of those evangelicals are Pentecostal.[2] While many social scientists (including Peter Berger, Paul Freston, and Elizabeth Brusco) have documented the changes experienced by women within their families and churches due to the rise of evangelicalism and pluralism, there has been little exploration of evangelicalism and pluralism's joint impacts on women's political lives, something this chapter seeks to address.

With Berger, I suspect that pluralism is good for faith. Brazilian women exercise new choices within the context of a culture that is strongly religious and strongly secular, yet one that continues to retain gendered family expectations that make women's status and prospects in the public sphere of particular interest to me as a political scientist. When traveling to Brazil in fall 2015, I saw firsthand that the political, economic and social shifts had resulted in an increasingly democratic, capitalist, and pluralist society. These shifts have enabled some women to garner leadership in the church and society, although it remains to be seen if the majority of women could experience the benefits of such empowerment. Specifically, I explore if the impact of modernization in the public and private spheres empowers women to make choices with the support of church or family, or whether women who exercise their choice feel marginalized, cheated of the benefits of their empowerment because they have to pay such a high price for undertaking them. In the current political context of Brazil, I ask whether pluralism is indeed good for women of faith, some of whom have made choices to abandon one religious home for another, others of whom have taken leadership positions in church, society and the political arena, and still others who appear to be left behind.

To answer this question of marginalization or empowerment, I carried out semi-structured interviews in São Paulo and Maringá, Brazil, with the help of an experienced translator (Naama Mendes, Jr.). Fourteen participants in these interviews were undergraduate women seminarians (five at the University of São Paulo FATIPI campus and nine at Unicesumar in Maringá); one was a female sociologist at the Catholic University of São Paulo; and one was a female journalist at Valor Econômico, Brazil's largest financial newspaper. I also interviewed a married political couple—one a city councilwoman and one a state representative—in São Paulo. With

2. U.S. State Department, "Brazil."

the exception of the sociologist, everyone I interviewed is a self-identified evangelical Christian.

These interviews support the "Pentecostal gender bargain" described as the negotiations that many women engage in when they become evangelical and in particular when they become Pentecostal.[3] Participation in faith communities can offer some improvements in women's life circumstances—e.g., possibilities for leadership experiences, husbands taking on more responsibilities in the household—but at the cost of submission to ongoing forms of patriarchy within the church and their families, patterns I will document in the pages that follow. The question of whether evangelical women thrive both spiritually and socio-politically in the pluralist context does not have a simple answer. The picture is mixed, with costs as well as gains. The gains are significant: models of strong evangelical women in leadership are increasingly emerging, and, in this context, many—especially those with powerful family and church bonds—may yet succeed in creating new patterns that defy old stereotypical divides between secularist/elitist feminism and between secular women and women of orthodox religious commitments.

I will address two primary themes here. First, the role of modernity in enabling more choices and opportunities for women's engagement, yet simultaneously narrowing their options as it emphasizes individualism to the neglect of family and the common good. Second, the role of the church in enabling more choices and opportunities for a broad spectrum of women, offering them agency and a moral foundation for their empowerment, yet simultaneously limiting them to inferior positions and failing to fully embrace the church's social responsibilities. I conclude that women's participation in the political arena may be more egalitarian than in evangelical churches, but that women's inclusion in politics has lacked significant moral foundation, which leaves women's advancement inconsistent and troubled. I document that churches serve as major sources of empowerment for women, but also that women's gender both frees and limits them in this context. In the process, I conclude that the gender bargaining of Brazilian evangelical women takes place in a generally supportive modernizing context that nevertheless overvalues individualism, and a cultural context of machismo and materialism, against which the church provides women a moral compass and opportunities for leadership, at least in some cases, in the context of family support and more egalitarian family roles.

3. Martin, "Tensions and Trends," 128.

Women's Roles in Contemporary Brazil

The Brazilian Political, Economic, and Social Context

The broader Brazilian political, economic, and social context is a complicated one, with promises and perils for evangelical women. Brazil is a country of great possibilities, a member of the BRIC nations, and a top-ten world economy that successfully increased the size of its middle class from 38 percent to 50 percent since 2003, and has experienced more than 30 years of democratic rule after the military dictatorship. Yet Brazil's is a fragile democracy wracked by various economic, political, and social struggles.[4] Positively, it is a rising regional and global leader, hosting the World Cup in 2014, and the Olympics in 2016, leading developing nations within the WTO, and serving as a significant player within the G20 and the UN. It has a diversified economy, diverse trade partners, and a well-recognized, commonly emulated conditional cash transfer program (*Bolsa Família*) seeking to address poverty.[5] Yet Brazil has a long way to go in comprehensively redressing economic, racial, and gender inequalities, thwarting violent crime, and ameliorating the consequences of comparatively weak investment in public education in the past. Politically, it suffers from the burden of a massive, expensive, and an often non-meritocratic bureaucracy, contributing to wasted public expenditures and corruption.[6] Furthermore, it has fragmented political parties, which are kept weak in part by an open party-list proportional representation electoral system (where voters help determine the order in which candidates are elected). This electoral process helps keep candidates non-loyal to parties; candidates often run more as personalities than as members of parties, and sometimes don't even identify their parties in campaigns. In addition, in a typical legislative term, more than one-third of legislators will switch parties;[7] this makes party cohesion, loyalty, and discipline very difficult to muster. And this contributes to the frequent creation of new parties (Brazil has over twenty parties). Presidents and legislators must rely on weak multiparty coalitions to govern. Lack of cohesion and loyalty contributes to presidential circumvention of the chaotic legislature via the use of undemocratic executive decrees and/or a willingness to rely on unethical means to garner support for legislation (patronage, or

---

4. Siqueira Wiarda, "Brazil"; Skidmore et al., "Brazil"; Melkonian-Hoover, "Brazil's Winning Bid."
5. Shifter and Combs, "Shifting Fortunes."
6. Siqueira Wiarda, "Brazil," 118.
7. Power, "Brazilian Democracy at Twenty," 11; Rohter, *Brazil on the Rise*, 256.

resources and jobs).[8] This contributes to and helps explain all too frequent corruption practices and scandals.[9]

Currently Brazil is in the midst of serious economic and political crises, a difficult context for any aspiring reformer, not least those who are evangelical women. Economically, Brazil suffered the downgrading of its national debt to junk status in February 2016, a 45 percent depreciation of its currency, the *real*, from 2014 to 2016, amid popular doubts regarding the excessive costs of the 2014 World Cup and 2016 Rio Olympics. It has also experienced a public health emergency due to the proliferation of the Zika virus since 2015, a mosquito-borne disease that causes microcephaly in newborns.[10] In March 2015 Petrobras (the state-owned oil company) and President Rousseff's Worker's Party/PT were implicated in a massive corruption scandal (*Lava Jato* or Operation Car Wash) in which the PT took billions of dollars in kickbacks on government contracts for Petrobras to support its campaigns. Implicitly due to frustration with the *Lava Jato*, and explicitly due to her creative budget practices/fiscal maneuvers to hide the extent of Brazil's significant public debt, in May 2016 the legislature voted to suspend President Dilma Rousseff to undergo an impeachment trial.[11]

Despite the complicated impeachment process of Brazil's first female president, it's important to recall Brazil has not only successfully elected a female president, but multiple female governors, legislators, and mayors. Women's empowerment and opportunities have been varied over the last century, contributing to an uneven context for evangelical women's civic/political engagement. By 1932, women in Brazil already had the vote, and women's equality was enshrined in the Brazilian constitution of 1988 (Article 5.I). In addition, women also fought for and won the constitutional right to a maternity leave of 120 days (Article 7.XVIII) and established an indeterminate paternity leave (Article 7.XIX).[12] At the same time, however, Brazilians are known for their machismo attitudes, namely presumptions of masculine superiority and privilege.[13] As in the U.S., women in Brazil

---

8. Power, "Brazilian Democracy at Twenty."
9. Rohter, *Brazil on the Rise.*
10. Taylor, "Five Upsides."
11. Rousseff was a protégée and former chief of staff of the popular previous president Lula da Silva, *BBC News*, "What Has Gone Wrong."
12. Alvarez, *Engendering Democracy.*
13. Salek, "How Rousseff Has Highlighted Brazil's Sexism Problem."

still have lesser access to employment, earn less, and are expected to take on more passive roles within relationships than men.[14]

On the whole, it is clear that Brazil has been modernizing over the last few decades, experiencing the pluralism that Berger describes, giving women more options religiously, socially, economically, and politically. Brazil is a promising country but is currently experiencing extensive turmoil, requiring significant reform to evade further dilemmas and deterioration, and the status of women varies considerably.

In this context, I interviewed evangelical women leaders and seminarians,[15] asking these individuals to talk about their leadership experience; how gender affects evangelical women's engagement in private and public life in an increasingly pluralist Brazil; and how women navigate, as Berger puts it in the opening chapter of this book, the shift from fate to choice.

Negotiating the Family

The private sphere traditionally has been a primary area of focus for many women, with religion reinforcing (if not outright forcing) this focus. But modern evangelicalism might in some ways help women resist marginalization and enable the reformation of machismo as Latin American scholars Cecília Loreto Mariz, Elizabeth Brusco, and others attest.[16]

These interviews revealed mixed perceptions and experiences for women in Brazil today. Sociologist Claudirene Bandini told us her research indicates that women pastors in top positions experience some increased autonomy outside the family sphere because of their particular status. To be sure, on the whole, they experience ongoing dilemmas regarding lack of childcare and lack of help in the home—dilemmas common to most Brazilian women. However, because of their status, women in these positions are able to negotiate with husbands to pursue things outside of marriage and be more autonomous, enabling greater mobility. This appears to be the case not because men are taking up more of the private sphere responsibilities, but because both wives and husbands are able to hire others to help them.

14. Rohter, *Brazil on the Rise*, 52.

15. The trip was led by Dr. Kaye Cook and conducted with faculty colleague Dr. Sharon Ketcham.

16. Brusco, *The Reformation of Machismo*; Mariz, *Coping with Poverty*; Burdick, *Looking for God in Brazil*; Drogus, "Religious Change and Women's Status in Latin America."

As for broader implications, Bandini noted that sometimes these women reach down to bring other women up and help free and encourage them as well.[17]

Most of the female seminarians with whom we spoke did not see a contradiction between their pursuit of ministry and their commitment to family, supposing the ability to pursue both. During our interview with nine female seminarians at Unicesumar in Maringá, only one ("Seminarian B") was willing to call herself a complementarian; the others considered themselves egalitarians. Generally speaking, egalitarians are those who contend that women and men should have equal roles within the family, church, and society, while complementarians contend women and men have distinct responsibilities to fulfill within those realms.[18] Given this need for complementarity, Seminarian B said she'd have to be married to serve in the church: "If someone called me to a certain area, I wouldn't accept. I would wait on God to have someone accompany me."[19]

Although some women felt resistance to serve, on the whole these seminarians felt spiritual confirmation of their pursuit of ministry. During this same conversation, Seminarian A said she had perceived a lot of resistance in her church and in her society toward women being at the same level as men; Brazilian women historically have been pressured to stay at home, she reported, especially among the poorest classes. But after studying Scriptures herself, she came to believe that women have a fundamental role in ministry and in all positions. And all nine of the women affirmed they felt called by the Holy Spirit to study theology.

A contemporary example of an evangelical couple simultaneously pursuing their public callings and care of their family is that of well-known São Paulo politicians Patrícia and Carlos Bezzera. They have the experience of being professionals (a psychologist and obstetrician-gynecologist, respectively), ordained ministers, politicians, and co-parents to their children, both seeking to fulfill their calls in the public and private spheres. It has not been an easy path, however. Carlos entered politics twelve years before Patrícia did, and as one of their colleagues mentioned to us, in order to disprove that she got elected on Carlos' coattails, Patrícia had to work

17. Claudirene Bandirini, interview by author, São Paulo, Brazil, August 9, 2015. See also Lula Garcia-Navarro, "Which Place Is More Sexist?," who notes that Brazil experiences the seventh highest rate of violence against women in the world.

18. Warnock, "Gender."

19. Unicesumar Seminarians, interview by author and Dr. Kaye Cook, Maringá, Brazil, August 14, 2015.

harder to prove she earned the right to be a politician.[20] While the costs appear to be greater for Patrícia than Carlos, Patrícia has been able to pursue her political call, ministry, *and* familial care.

One disturbing addendum to these shifts in family relations is that women still too often experience abuse in the private sphere. Politician Patrícia Bezerra has made women's issues her top priority, particularly violence against women; she has developed programs to address sexual violence. As journalist Marília de Camargo César shared with us, it is estimated that over half of evangelical women in Brazil are victims of domestic violence.[21] This may be in part related to the dilemma that evangelicals are disproportionately poor and thus possess fewer options,[22] and more women than men practice the faith.[23] To be sure, it is not clear that increased religiosity or that women's engagement in ministry or the public sphere in general contribute to these startling statistics. One sign of hope shared by Camargo César is that an important women's NGO (*Instituto Mulher Viva*) has begun working cooperatively with an evangelical coalition (the *Aliança Cristã Evangélica*) to address this problem.[24]

On the whole, evangelical women, at least those in positions of influence, appear to be experiencing greater sharing of responsibilities within the domestic sphere by both sexes, given the emphasis on the family within the faith. Such sharing helps decrease women's marginalization, and enables them to increase their engagement in other spheres. As well, an increasing number of evangelical women are pursuing church ministry alongside family life. Although evangelical women still struggle with machismo and abuse, these concerns do seem to be increasingly acknowledged, and there are growing political, NGO, and church efforts to reform machismo and fight the scourge of domestic violence. In addition, seminary women we interviewed are emboldened to enter new territories with or without husbands, moving from fate to choice—something unimaginable only a few decades ago. Further research would be needed to analyze in depth what dynamic these future religious leaders foresee between their personal and

---

20. Patrícia and Carlos Bezerra, interview by author, Wenham, MA, September 14, 2015; Carlos Bezerra, interview by author, São Paulo, Brazil, August 11, 2015.

21. Marília de Camargo César, interview by author and Dr. Kaye Cook, São Paulo, Brazil, August 10, 2015.

22. True, *The Political Economy*.

23. Hefner, "The Unexpected Modern," 11.

24. Marília de Camargo César.

ministry roles. In my interviews, few shared their thoughts about family issues, or highlighted major positive transformations. However, their very presence within these seminaries, albeit still a minority presence, signals the potential for a future sea change.

Navigating the Church

Moving outside of the home and into the community, it is important to explore how—and if—the church experience itself has been transformative for evangelical women in Brazil. As scholars such as Nanlai Cao have noticed in other regions, women in evangelical and Pentecostal churches in Brazil are often presumed to be more spiritually inclined than men, while men are presumed to be more theologically gifted and sophisticated than women. Often, the result has been limited teaching opportunities for women.[25] Yet there are reasons to expect that many will find the tools to resist patriarchy from within the church, embracing new choices.

Unlike the Catholic Church, which has struggled with a shortage of priests within Latin America, evangelical churches can proliferate quickly and under a range of leaders (seminary trained and/or Spirit directed), within any neighborhood imaginable.[26] In the poorest and/or newest of neighborhoods, it is evangelical churches that establish themselves immediately. That means Protestant churches are increasingly accessible institutions for women in all walks of life, and they are well situated to meet needs and effect change. Based on our interviews, it appears many churches have committed to women's accessibility, but struggle with reinforcing gender discrimination.

Politician Patrícia Bezerra's life exemplifies new opportunities available to women within Protestantism in Brazil. She is part of an independent neo-Pentecostal church that broke away from the Foursquare Gospel Church (a denomination that was founded by a woman).[27] Although Bezerra voiced frustration with ongoing limits and sexism in her new church, she noted women not only can pray in her church, but can actually preach; and she herself is an ordained minister in it.

---

25. Cao, "Gender, Modernity and Pentecostal Christianity in China."

26. Interview with Samuel Escobar by John Allen, "The Dramatic Growth of Evangelicals in Latin America"; Pew Research Center, David Masci interview with Andrew Chesnut, "Why Has Pentecostalism Grown So Dramatically in Latin America?"

27. Aimee Semple McPherson founded the denomination in 1923 in Los Angeles.

As for would-be female church leaders, most expressed optimism regarding new opportunities for women: eight of the nine Unicesumar theology students in Maringá said they felt free to pursue further education (a master's or doctorate degree). Most were in denominations that ordain women, and only one (B) was outspoken against women's ordination. Seminarian B said she disagreed with most of her female cohort and thinks women have a traditional role to take care of the family, and to help out rather than lead independently; she feared the emotional component of pastoral work might be too much for the female. The women at Unicesumar noted that in one of their theology classes a conversation took place about whether or not women should be theologians; some male students said they should not. But some of these women complained during our interview that when male students needed help with coursework, they felt free to rely on the women. This hints at possibilities that with increasing access to theological training, women will have greater access to teaching roles within congregations, or conversely, that men will simply rely on their knowledge while claiming the pulpit. "I think things are changing. In the past, women couldn't do anything. Now they can do everything: pastor, pray, serve in all ministries. They are leaders," shared Seminarian C. In contrast to B's perspective and experience, Seminarian C worshipped under a female head pastor who encouraged C's theological studies and financially supported her training. Another seminarian remarked that although there is still a lot of machismo in the church and in society, God is raising up both women and men to preach.[28]

Within the São Paulo seminary (FATIPI), the sentiment of the female seminarians was similar, if not even more progressive. Women's ordination was increasingly presumed and yet with it has come a mixed array of opportunities for women. Seminarian D said, "Ordaining females is maybe a controversy of the past. Today the controversy is LGBT issues and how to deal with that in the appropriate manner."[29] FATIPI professor Shirley Proença disagreed; she said that while the seminary is at the forefront of the movement to promote gender equality, the issue of female ordination is not settled. Echoing Proença's concern, Seminarian E said that when a husband and wife work together as a pastoral team, "[there is] difficulty for the church to accept both pastors as having equal say in the leadership of

28. Unicesumar Seminarians.

29. FATIPI Seminarians, interview by author and Dr. Kaye Cook, São Paulo, Brazil, August 10, 2015.

the church.... Usually the female becomes the auxiliary pastor... and a lot are not paid for their services." In the Assemblies of God denomination in Brazil, journalist Camargo César noted, it is common practice that "wives of pastors are nominated *pastoras* in fact but not in right." Wives of male ministers are ordained as ministers as well, but typically they do not preach on Sundays, although they may heal and lead many ministries within the church.[30] Camargo César identified neo-Pentecostal churches as the ones in which women find the most significant roles. "*Pastoras* have real power within these churches and in some cases compete with and dispute the power of their *pastor* husbands" she said.[31] And here as well, women are often more engaged in prophetic and healing ministries than in teaching ministries, though not exclusively so.

On the whole, FATIPI seminarians shared the Unicesumar seminarians' guarded optimism regarding changing opportunities for women to be ordained and serve within congregations and society, even if women's and men's posts within congregations aren't always equal. But limitations remain. Two FATIPI seminarians of color from the Northeast (a poorer, rural, and heavily Afro-Brazilian region of Brazil) highlighted that in that region, the view of gender roles remains more traditional. Seminarian F commented, "In my church, there are no female elders.... And so I see that if I'm here today it was because God desired for it to be so... I believe that the church of God is not limited within these four walls."[32]

Sociologist Bandini told me that having significant family capital/status can help women move beyond church constraints or, more particularly, out of the shadows and into the spotlight as *lead* pastors. Evangelical ecclesiastical space is not as democratic as is often claimed; it is subject to political and financial incentives and pressures, a scenario that women with family capital often use to their advantage. The advantages these few women can accrue may come with serious costs for women and men. According to several people we interviewed, inequities and abuses of power are especially common in Brazilian churches focused on the prosperity ("health and wealth") gospel, problems that have been on the rise for some time, particularly within Pentecostalism. These churches are often marked by corruption and a lack of accountability, Camargo César and others told me. As in political life, in church governance the concentration of power

30. Marília de Camargo César.
31. Ibid.
32. FATIPI Seminarians.

in a sole executive creates significant room for abuse. On the whole, this understandably constrains the capacity of the church to facilitate women's (and men's) progress.

Within evangelical churches in Brazil, opportunities for women to lead and preach may be growing. Across denominations, the trend is toward the ordination of women, but women's leadership roles are not always *in front*: as noted, women pastors more often focus on prayer, prophecy, and healing than on theology and teaching. A woman's family connections may help her overcome patriarchal bias, as may the support for (and increase of) women training to be church leaders themselves. Finally, and unsurprisingly, lack of accountability and corruption within congregations impedes progress for most parishioners, including women, constraining the capacity of the church to transform women's positions and assist them in moving from fate to choice.

Venturing Out into Society and Politics

One of the most significant findings of this study is the idea that evangelical women in Brazil are drawing resources from within the faith and from modernity to move beyond personal transformation and church engagement to broader social and political transformation and engagement. Even while cognizant of significant changes in the public sphere, many scholars, including the highly regarded sociologist of religion Paul Freston, express skepticism regarding evangelical political engagement. This is due in part to significant divisions within Protestantism, and the simplistic approach taken by many evangelical politicians who are often new to the political arena, making them easy targets for corruption and manipulation.[33] On the whole, these interviews reveal a healthy skepticism about outspoken Christian politicians, alongside a budding optimism about effective social and political engagement by women.

Protestant churches in Brazil are well situated to engage in social and political transformation and meet acute needs. As journalist Camargo César highlighted, evangelical churches are widespread and actively involved in their communities; people are available during the week, offering a range of religious and social services such as Bible studies and literacy classes. These churches' extensive lay leadership and their focus on practical concerns, not just abstract political ideas, enables more pastoral intervention

33. Freston, "Introduction"; Hefner, "The Unexpected Modern."

(in contrast to the work of the Catholic Church, which often lacks sufficient priests to be readily available for such practical engagement). For instance, an important program in Camargo César's evangelical church is its literacy program, which steps in where the government's public schools are failing. This has been particularly crucial given that the lowest classes cannot afford private education; it gives churches the opportunity to meet a desperate societal need and offer an after-school alternative to violence on the streets.[34] Even so, literacy programs run by churches are unfortunately not that common, and tend to focus their efforts on adults.

A number of seminarians initiated discussion of ways their congregations are similarly and importantly addressing felt needs, moving parishioners out of the pews and into the streets to effect change. Seminarian D at FATIPI in São Paulo noted her call to ministry of bringing the church into the community through the NGO in which she works, an NGO situated within a large *favela*, or low-income, historically informal urbanized area. She said what really matters is "the inclusion of the church in society: being able to keep up with society and seeing the social movements that are going on in society and how the church can address that in a meaningful manner."[35] Seminarian F noted that in her city of Sorocaba, in the state of São Paulo, she does not see any state organization dealing with adolescents and females that have just left the prison system. This is a gap within civil society that the church has at times led the way in responding to, offering care to some of the most vulnerable women.

At Unicesumar in Maringá, seminary women generally agreed that recent shifts for women in the church and in society would result in women being more engaged politically as well, and for the greater good. As seminarian G said, women can help clean up society ("[because] we're mothers, care [for others] is closer to us"), echoing maternal feminist language.[36] Politician Patrícia Bezerra herself exemplifies this call, as a psychologist, mother, and pastor who's moved into the political sphere to help transform and reform society. An evangelical politician, Bezerra focuses her political work on addressing injustices against women and mothers given the considerable discrimination they face in Brazilian society. In addition to combatting violence against women, she supports women's right to breastfeed

---

34. Menjívar, "Religion and Immigration in Comparative Perspective."
35. FATIPI Seminarians.
36. Gilligan, *In A Different Voice*; Ruddick, *Maternal Thinking*.

in public, and advocates for poor women's right to have anesthesia during childbirth.[37]

Other evangelical women politicians are similarly seeking to transform society and make institutional reforms in Brazil, inspired by faith and encouraging others to similarly respond. Such is the case with the well-known environmental activist Marina Silva, a two-time presidential candidate who has served in the Brazilian Senate and as Minister of the Environment. Camargo César is a biographer of the politician.[38] Silva believes since God is creator of this world it is our responsibility to care for God's creation, but she gets accused of being a fundamentalist for turning to faith in addition to science (although she does not, for example, support a literal six-day creation). Connections between faith and politics for her and other evangelicals are key. Silva observes:

> I would say the evangelical churches are just beginning to make the connection between the ethical principles of Christianity and the principles that would guide our actions in secular life. There are several people who are starting to say: "Look, it's not just a question of ethics from the moral point of view." This ethics also has to be in our relationship to public institutions . . . .[39]

Silva doesn't switch gears and secularize/neutralize her faith when functioning as a politician in a pluralistic society (a gear-switching that Berger presumes is the typical coping mechanism for strong religionists functioning in public space). Faith is clearly an animating, driving force for her political engagement as a marginalized Afro-Brazilian woman rising up out of poverty. She bemoans the fact that the church has been slow to make these links, but commends the change that is arising.

Unfortunately, not all churches are on board with this vision and many of the evangelicals who do enter politics have not heeded the call to reform the political system, often succumbing to structural temptations and/or falling into the trap of fixating upon the polarizing culture wars to attract fearful voters. Many of the politically engaged women I interviewed expressed concern about the record of evangelicals in contemporary Brazilian politics; many of the first evangelicals in the 1980s who did become national legislators were paid off by the government in the form of bribes

---

37. Patrícia Bezerra.
38. Camargo César, *Entre a Cruz e o Arco-Íris* (*Between the Cross and the Rainbow*).
39. Fonseca, "Religion and Democracy in Brazil," 181.

and broadcasting concessions.⁴⁰ In my interview with journalist Camargo César, she worried that average evangelicals remain naïve politically and therefore are easily influenced by hardline conservative evangelical politicians. The *Bancada Evangelica* (Evangelical Front), a coalition of conservative politicians elected in 2010, focuses primarily on abortion, marriage, and culture wars, to the neglect of education and inequality issues. In 2015, it held over 70 of Brazil's 513 legislative seats. Some of its top leaders, such as former Speaker of the House, Eduardo Cunha, have been implicated in recent corruption scandals.⁴¹ Seminarian D of FATIPI in São Paulo said that as a Christian she is embarrassed that "there is an extremely fundamentalist, right wing agenda of the Evangelical Front that has a disturbed view of the Gospel that does not reflect the love of Christ." She believes that "the job of the Church, at least the Presbyterian Church, has not been to condemn, but rather to . . . bring in, and try to attract people in that way."⁴²

On the whole, however, public engagement by Brazilian Christians is diversifying; Brazilian Christians are engaged in political parties across the spectrum, and increasingly concerned not simply with personal moral issues or church-related issues, but also with structural concerns and societal ills. Women may be well positioned to enter the fray and parlay personal transformation into political transformation. As the prominent sociologist of religion Robert Hefner asserts:

> Notwithstanding a tendency to retreat from structural engagements where these carry high social costs, the Pentecostal experience in Latin America [and in Brazil in particular, where, he notes, *all* parties have evangelical candidates] hints at a remarkable global possibility. It suggests the Pentecostal preoccupation with ethical-subject reformation need not end in antipolitics or quietist retreat from the public sphere. The ethical self may extend its gaze to structural and social justice concerns, not least of all where politics is no longer an elite-dominated, zero-sum game.⁴³

40. Ibid.

41. Eduardo Cunha, a Brazilian politician and a leading figure in the Evangelical Bancada, was deeply involved in the 2016 effort to impeach President Dilma Rousseff; in mid-2016 the Brazilian Supreme Court suspended Cunha from his role as speaker of the lower house due to corruption charges related to the *Lava Jato*/Car Wash Petrobras scandal, http://www.huffingtonpost.com/diego-iraheta/eduardo-cunha-ciao-darlin_b_9852394.html.

42. FATIPI Seminarians.

43. Hefner, *Global Pentecostalism*, 19.

It is clear that many of the evangelical women we interviewed see society, even politics, as a mission field; they feel inspired and affirmed by churches and the Holy Spirit to engage the public square and fill in the gaps. But they are also worried about the reputation of evangelicals in politics, particularly the Evangelical Front, with its focus on marriage and life issues over and above poverty concerns. Many recognize the difficulty of entering a political system in which patronage is entrenched, and the difficulties of governing effectively and ethically within it.[44] As Patrícia's husband and São Paulo Congressman Carlos Bezerra highlighted, there is a need for humility, mentors, accountability, and reformation of a corrupt system to advance and sustain the legitimate role of Christians in politics.[45] And he reminded us of Martin Luther King Jr.'s admonition that "the church is not the master or the servant of the state but rather the conscience of the state."[46]

Skeptics have legitimate reservations; the political system is challenging and evangelicals have not always fared well within it. Evangelical women's public engagement thus far is admittedly not extensive. Still, the fact that Brazilian politics is in the midst of crisis may actually create a political opportunity for evangelicals—and women evangelicals are well positioned to enter the political sphere, as they are often perceived as fresh, uncorrupted candidates able to step in, clean up, and address structural and social concerns. A common orientation across my diverse interviewees was a reformist outlook. If (when) this perspective gets a stronger foothold in Brazilian public affairs, it may, for example, help bring about electoral reforms that would make it difficult to jump parties or campaign reforms to limit the influence of special interests—all of which could help create more virtuous cycles within the political system, combatting the structural mechanisms that contribute to corruption.

Is Pluralism Good for Evangelical Women in Brazil?

Women's gender appears to both free and limit them; modernity and the rise of pluralism is insufficient to eradicate the influence of machismo in

---

44. Alexandre Fonseca notes many of the first evangelicals to enter politics in Brazil fell into corruption; yet he also points to examples of many (including Bezerra and Silva) who are carving out new spaces in the center and on the left ("Religion and Democracy in Brazil").

45. Carlos Bezerra.

46. King, "A Knock at Midnight."

Brazilian society, while the church also has a mixed record in this regard. For many of these women, modernity and its developments are translated through their faith and the church; some liberalizing elements are adopted, others rejected, and others deftly nuanced. For example, human sexuality and practice has been a key and ongoing tension between the church and modern Brazilian society, a tension that many of these women leaders seek to address (Camargo César herself has written an important text on the matter).[47]

In terms of addressing gender divisions and facilitating equality, modernity is slow in generating egalitarian effects among evangelical women in Brazil, at times because of its own limitations and at times, stymied by certain facets of the church. Modernity with its focus on individual human rights helps women lobby for their individual advancement. Yet it also narrows in decidedly on individual needs and the freedom to pursue such, so much so that it can feed into hyper individualism and consumerism to the neglect of community and the common good. As well, even positive modern impulses may be limited by the religious traditions of these evangelicals; the majority of evangelical women are still Pentecostals and Baptists, denominational groups that, according to journalist Camargo César, "are still a long way from holding their women as equally empowered with their male [counter]parts."[48] Exacerbating this, as Seminarian H of FATIPI in São Paulo stressed, in the Northeast of Brazil, "machismo is still very, very much part of the culture. So women have been constantly breaking those barriers in the Northeast, including two female pastors in my city that have broken through . . . [yet] they still are seen as different by other pastors . . . [but] what I have seen is that each time that I go back, the churches are not as closed as they were before but they're more open to female leadership." In her region it appears her church may play a key role in moving society along on questions of gender equity and access. And yet another student from the Northeast, Seminarian I, part of a conservative Assemblies of God congregation, shared: "I think [egalitarian leadership] is all very new. . . . there's not this lust or ambition [of women] to be a pastor in our church. The roles for leadership [there] are not open to us, and our roles are very predetermined as females."

Many seminarians I interviewed have been deeply invested in considering how to navigate modernity well as Christians, and as Christian

---

47. Camargo César, *Entre a Cruz e o Arco-Íris* (*Between the Cross and the Rainbow*).

48. Marília de Camargo César.

women in particular. While churches may not always be explicitly egalitarian and may not directly combat machismo in the pulpit, in practice, many churches play an empowering role in women's lives in pushing them into the public sphere. Seminarian B of Unicesmar in Maringá raised the following: "Many churches have activities that keep us in the church. But one of the missions of my church is to decentralize the church and take people to the streets, to be able to supplement civil society."[49] There is a commitment to moving outward, not just inward. Even when students expressed frustration with others for being inwardly focused, they had a sense that their own congregations were shifting outward, and "doing this right." As Seminarian A noted, "My pastor has said, 'You are a missionary wherever you are; your mission field is your job, your family, the people around you.' He also promotes more intimacy with God, more time reading the Bible, more time praying, more time with the Holy Spirit. That being so, if you're intimate with the Lord, you'll be able to walk in the Spirit." For her, deep personal transformation necessarily leads to effective social transformation. This affirms sociologist of religion Bernice Martin's argument regarding the agency that evangelicalism can offer to mobilize populations, women in particular, in the modern world.[50] This faith-inspired agency can help women take advantage of modern norms that elevate choice over fate.

In addition to a sense of agency, churches—even undemocratic ones—can offer particular kinds of access and mobility to women that feminist groups are not always privy to. Sociologist Bandini remarked to us, "Non-Christian feminism is built by rich white women in ivory-tower universities, so there's not real effectiveness to it. Christian feminism is more involved in the civil society and has real praxis."[51] Many feminist movements in Brazil have had the reputation of being elitist and focused primarily on issues of abortion and sexuality, sometimes to the neglect of economic, labor, and family concerns.[52] In addition, sociologist Bandini confirms that feminist scholars don't tend to do well with issues of marriage or family, often ignoring or dismissing rather than wrestling with them, failing to address them while churches take such issues seriously. Again, modern liberalism helpfully values the individual and individual rights, but often at the cost of relationships and group interests.

49. Unicesumar Seminarians.
50. Martin, "Tensions and Trends."
51. Claudirene Bandini.
52. Alvarez, *Engendering Democracy in Brazil*.

Within churches, Bandini notes, marriage and family, while acknowledged and explored, can also be understood in limiting ways. Being single and not having children can thwart women's capacity to develop into leadership. However, women in the church can use marriage and motherhood, if they manage them well, to support their advancement within church ministry. And the church can help women consider how to develop, enhance, and negotiate those identities as well, not simply view all of life through the lens of one's individual status.

The church can offer a foundation for women's equality and engagement that modernity lacks. To be sure, many Brazilian women have relied on modern developments and others, on the church to facilitate greater gender inclusion, equality, and engagement. Simultaneously, some have found the work of the church crucial to resisting the pressures of modern society regarding gender. As Brazil is experiencing today on the national political stage, women's inclusion in politics has lacked significant moral foundation; it rests on uncertain ground, with sexism and machismo ever pervasive. As of 2018, interim president Michel Temer, the replacement for female president Dilma Rousseff while she undergoes impeachment proceedings, had yet to appoint a woman (or a person of color) to his cabinet.[53] And former PT president Luiz Lula da Silva, a mentor to Rousseff, was caught on tape speaking of women in debased, vulgar, and dehumanizing ways in recordings released in 2016.[54]

The church appears to have something substantive to offer in advancing women in more than the status quo's tenuous and hyper-individualistic manner. It can support women's inclusion, and the inclusion of all, situated within the context of community, based on a respect for humanity created in the image of God, and understood as equally valued, worthy, and equipped to serve.

Conclusion

As Bernice and David Martin attest, evangelicalism, and Pentecostalism in particular, seems more modernizing than not on the whole, as it can support and facilitate increased engagement in multiple spheres in an increasingly liberalized society.[55] And this is true for women as well as men,

53. Salek, "How Rousseff Has Highlighted Brazil's Sexism Problem."
54. Garcia-Navarro, "In Brazilian Officials' Taped Conversations."
55. Martin, "Tensions and Trends."

even if the paths for women and men differ. The church is arguably better positioned to make key changes for large numbers of women than are elite feminist organizations with little reach or access to the majority of the population. But what is the church doing with that access? The current and future leaders I interviewed desire to see the church grow in its commitment to fight domestic abuse. They believe the church should support men taking on greater responsibilities in the private sphere, and should promote and support women and the use of their gifts and talents in the church and in society. These current and future leaders are motivated to fight corruption in the church, society, and governance. They want the church to take seriously its role as a voice of conscience to society and government, and to vigilantly avoid becoming conflated with political power. Thus far, the record is mixed; women have submitted to forms of the "Pentecostal gender bargain"; e.g., accepting secondary posts in churches, maintaining disproportionate responsibility within the private sphere, and perhaps biding their time for political engagement, and yet the potential for progress is significant.

Likewise, the record of modernity itself is mixed. The complex reality of modernity in Brazil today, which does indeed feature the kind of deep pluralism discussed by Peter Berger (one with space for *all* voices, including a powerful secular discourse alongside diverse religious ones), creates the space for religious women yet simultaneously resists religious contributions to women's flourishing, given its continued reliance on sexist and corrupting structures, its preference for the individual versus the community, and the common secularist bias against conservative religious discourse and engagement.

Ultimately, based on these interviews, it is clear that evangelical Brazilian women struggle with ongoing forms of marginalization, due in part to the church and due in part to modernity. The interviews also revealed positive signs and clear potential for women's increased inclusion and advancement because of the evangelical experience and its efficacy at helping women negotiate and engage modernity in stable and empowering ways. The path these women take within the private and public sphere is a complicated one, with perils to be sure. But considering Brazil's current rocky context, it is one that is surprisingly promising as well, one that will carry many from fate to choice, enabling individual and collective advancement.

Bibliography

Alvarez, Sonia. *Engendering Democracy in Brazil: Women's Movements in Transition Politics.* Princeton: Princeton University Press, 1990.

BBC News. "What Has Gone Wrong in Brazil?" May 31, 2016. http://www.bbc.com/news/world-latin-america-35810578.

Berger, Peter L. *The Desecularization of the World: Resurgent Religion and World Politics.* Grand Rapids: Eerdmans, 1999.

Brusco, Elizabeth. *The Reformation of Machismo: Evangelical Conversion and Gender in Colombia.* Austin: University of Texas Press, 1995.

Burdick, John. *Looking for God in Brazil: The Progressive Catholic Church in Urban Brazil's Arena.* Berkeley: University of California Press, 1993.

Camargo César, Marília de. *Entre a Cruz e o Arco-Íris (Between the Cross and the Rainbow).* São Paulo: Gutenberg, 2013.

Cao, Nanlai. "Gender, Modernity and Pentecostal Christianity in China." In *Global Pentecostalism in the 21st Century,* edited by Robert W. Hefner, 149–175. Bloomington: Indiana University Press, 2013.

César, Marília de Camargo. *Entre a Cruz e o Arco-Íris (Between the Cross and the Rainbow).* São Paulo: Gutenberg, 2013.

Drogus, Carol Ann. "Religious Change and Women's Status in Latin America: A Comparison of Christian Base Communities and Pentecostal Churches." *Kellogg Institute Working Paper #205:* March, 1994.

Escobar, Samuel. "The Dramatic Growth of Evangelicals in Latin America." Interview by John Allen, *National Catholic Reporter,* August 18, 2006, http://ncronline.org/blogs/all-things-catholic/dramatic-growth-evangelicals-latin-america.

Fonseca, Alexandre. "Religion and Democracy in Brazil: A Study of the Leading Evangelical Politicians." In *Evangelical Christianity and Democracy in Latin America,* edited by Paul Freston, 163–206. Oxford: Oxford University Press, 2008.

Freston, Paul. "Introduction: The Many Faces of Evangelical Politics in Latin America," in *Evangelical Christianity and Democracy in Latin America,* edited by Paul Freston, 3–36. Oxford: Oxford University Press, 2008.

Garcia-Navarro, Lula. "In Brazilian Officials' Taped Conversations, Women Hear Rampant Sexism." *Morning Edition (National Public Radio).* March 2, 2016. http://www.npr.org/sections/parallels/2016/03/22/471389523/in-brazilian-officials-taped-conversations-women-hear-rampant-sexism.

———. "Which Place Is More Sexist, the Middle East or Latin America?" *National Public Radio.* March 11, 2014. http://www.npr.org/sections/parallels/2014/03/11/289058115/which-place-is-more-sexist-the-middle-east-or-latin-america.

Gilligan, Carol. *In A Different Voice.* Cambridge, MA: Harvard University Press, 1982.

Hefner, Robert W., ed. *Global Pentecostalism in the 21st Century.* Bloomington: Indiana University Press, 2013.

Hefner, Robert W. "The Unexpected Modern: Gender, Piety and Politics in the Global Pentecostal Surge" in *Global Pentecostalism in the 21st Century,* edited by Robert W. Hefner, 1–36. Bloomington: Indiana University Press, 2013.

King, Martin Luther. "A Knock at Midnight." June 11, 1967. Sermon. http://kingencyclopedia.stanford.edu/encyclopedia/documentsentry/doc_a_knock_at_midnight.1.html.

Mariz, Cecilia Loreto. *Coping with Poverty: Pentecostals and Christian Base Communities in Brazil*. Philadelphia: Temple University Press, 1994.

Martin, Bernice. "Tensions and Trends in Pentecostal Gender and Family Relations," in *Global Pentecostalism in the 21st Century*, edited by Robert Hefner, 115–48. Bloomington: Indiana University Press, 2013.

Melkonian-Hoover, Ruth. "Brazil's Winning Bid Provides Olympic Lesson for the World." *Salem News*. November 25, 2009.

Menjívar, Cecilia. "Religion and Immigration in Comparative Perspective: Catholic and Evangelical Salvadorans in San Francisco, Washington, D.C. and Phoenix." *Sociology of Religion* 64 (2003) 21–45.

Pew Research Center. "Why Has Pentecostalism Grown So Dramatically in Latin America?" November 14, 2014. http://www.pewresearch.org/fact-tank/2014/11/14/why-has-pentecostalism-grown-so-dramatically-in-latin-america.

Power, Timothy. "Brazilian Democracy at Twenty." *Hemisphere: A Magazine of the Americas* 15 (Summer 2005) 10-13.

Rohter, Larry. *Brazil on the Rise: The Story of a Country Transformed*. New York: Palgrave Macmillan, 2012.

Ruddick, Sara. *Maternal Thinking: Towards a Politics of Peace*. Boston: Beacon, 1989.

Salek, Silvia. "How Rousseff Has Highlighted Brazil's Sexism Problem." *BBC News*. May 16, 2016. http://www.bbc.com/news/world-latin-america-36303001.

Shifter, Michael and Cameron Combs. "Shifting Fortunes: Brazil and Mexico in a Transformed Region." *Current History* 112 (February 2013) 49–55.

Siqueira Wiarda, Iêda. "Brazil: A Unique Country." In *Latin American Politics and Development*, edited by Howard Wiarda and Harvey Kline, 97–126. Boulder, CO: Westview, 2014.

Skidmore, Thomas E., Peter H. Smith, and James N. Green. "Brazil: The Awakening Giant," in *Modern Latin America*, 8th edition, edited by Skidmore et al., 296–340. Oxford: Oxford University Press, 2014.

Taylor, Matthew. "Five Upsides to Brazil's Crisis." Council on Foreign Relations. January 7, 2016.

True, Jacqui. *The Political Economy of Violence Against Women*. Oxford: Oxford University Press, 2012.

U.S. State Department. "Brazil." *International Religious Freedom Report*, 2014.

Warnock, Adrian. "Gender: Complementarian vs. Egalitarian Spectrum." *Patheos*. September 24, 2012. http://www.patheos.com/blogs/adrianwarnock/2012/09/gender-roles-a-complementarian-and-egalitarian-spectrum.

9

The Stranger's Address in Modernizing Cultures: Values and Pluralist Ideas among Brazilian and Chinese Christians

by Kaye V. Cook
Professor of Psychology

Si-Hua Chang

Taylor-Marie Funchion
Gordon College
Wenham, Massachusetts

Peter Berger describes two challenges of pluralism for Christian faith: the problem of secular spaces and the problem of pluralism's relativizing influence. Various authors in this volume (e.g., Wearne, Olson, and Skillen) challenge Berger's dualistic resolution of the problem of secular spaces, proposing instead an internal integrity that places all of the Christian experience under the lordship of Christ. Yet none challenge pluralism's relativizing influence, the focus of this chapter.[1]

By relativism, Berger means that modernization dramatically increases the sheer number of social constructions that an individual encounters,

---

1. Christian Smith (*Soul Searching, Souls in Transition*) has suggested a similarly relativistic phenomenon when he describes adolescents and emerging adults as having a watered-down rather than traditional Christian faith. A recent study by Kaye Cook, Chris Boyatzis, Cynthia Kimball, and Katherine Leonard (2015) documented that the relativizing phenomenon depends on the particular subculture under discussion and may be less extreme in highly religious contexts.

and this very multiplicity changes the nature of one's own social constructions, undermining certainty for people of faith. Berger further suggests that some of these new beliefs may be integrated into one's belief system in a process that he calls *cognitive contamination*. Our research in this closing chapter explores this relativizing influence from the perspective of individual experience, using the techniques of psychology.

Our choice to use psychological methods to describe personal faith permits analysis of the individual's experience in modernizing cultures and is consistent with the larger tradition that Berger's earlier writings have spawned. In their 1966 book *The Social Construction of Reality*,[2] Berger and Luckmann framed the concept of social constructionism. Reality, they argued, is no longer to be taken for granted or understood to be universal; rather, they wrote, reality is socially constructed by individuals living in culture who are simultaneously shaping culture while also being shaped by it. This bi-directional sociological construct has served as a bridge between the individual and the cultural, opening up new directions of thought throughout the human sciences. In the ensuing decades, the influence of social constructionism in psychology has manifested itself in narrative terms, focusing on the phenomenological and experiential realities of everyday, practical life from the perspective of the individuals themselves.[3]

Constructivist psychologists study narratives, believing that stories are individually constructed and socially embedded, and have the power to shape social phenomena.[4] Methods in constructivist psychology are thus designed to access individual stories, extracting constructions (i.e., generally phrases, though sometimes paragraphs if needed to capture the idea) from these stories that reveal how individuals understand the world.[5]

In traditional societies, it was not necessary to explore personal experience to describe one's faith, according to Berger. A person's physical address might have been, as he suggests, ancient Greece or Germany after World War II; their beliefs—whether in the many Olympian gods or the one Christian God—could be deduced from knowing where they lived. Berger uses the metaphorical term "the stranger's address" to denote the

---

2. Berger and Luckmann, *Social Construction of Reality*.
3. Crossley, "Formulating Narrative Psychology," 288–90.
4. Jovchelovitch and Bauer, "Narrative Interviewing."
5. Tashakkori et al., "Utilizing Mixed Methods," 429; Sandage, Cook, et al., "Hermeneutics and Psychology," 357; Cook et al., "Folk Conceptions of Virtue," 83–103.

common beliefs held by members of a culture, beliefs that classically accompanied their membership in that culture.

This identity between culture and belief system has, he argues, broken down in pluralist cultures, and one can no longer presume to know the beliefs of the other simply by knowing their country of residence. If we take Berger's observation seriously, perhaps indeed there is little to no relationship between one's beliefs and birthplace, a possibility we examine in our "values" study by asking whether Brazilian immigrants share values with other Brazilians, and Chinese immigrants with other Chinese.

Alternatively, in a pluralist culture, the voices of persons may show one's beliefs and birthplace but in a less homogeneous and more diverse way, revealing the day-to-day experience of living in modernizing worlds. We may hear in individual stories increasing echoes of the co-existence among "relevance structures"—socially derived environmental abstractions of experiences and events that are germane in the individual's lifeworld.[6] Relevance structures potentially refer to "religious actions and ideas," which, according to Berger, may "co-exist with secular ones, without necessarily colliding"; that is, without being internalized or even coming into conflict with one another. Coexistence may lead to cognitive contamination, or changes in beliefs and their underlying relevance structures. We agree with Berger that pluralism accompanies modernity. Further, we suggest that pluralist (or multiple) ideas coexisting in these interviews support his argument that pluralism, more common in modernizing than traditional societies, undermines certainty in faith. The presence of pluralist ideas gives quotidian evidence about how people deal with this complexity.

Following Berger's lead, we derived psychological measures for everyday examples in our interviews in which ideas come into conflict, whether internal ideas held in tension by one person or disagreements between two people or groups of people. In this chapter, therefore, we explore the belief systems of "others"—strangers, if you will—by interviewing participants from two modernizing countries. We ask whether we can locate these individuals by their birth culture, essentially asking if their culture serves as their address, and whether markers of modernity—i.e., the coexistence of multiple ideas that potentially undermine faith—can be identified.

---

6. Schutz and Luckmann, *The Structures of the Life-World*, 252–55.

Overview of Project

In our values study, we asked Brazilian and Chinese immigrants to list ten goals in their lives "right now" and to answer two life-review questions: "When you get toward the end of your life, what would you like to be able to say about your life looking back on it?" and "What values or beliefs do you think are the most important to pass on to the next generation?" From these lists of their goals, we identified the values (or guiding principles) that they currently pursue,[7] using the definitions of Shalom Schwartz in his cross-cultural research.[8] These values are described by their goals. The values include, for example, stimulation (whose goal is excitement, novelty, and challenge in life), benevolence (whose goal is preserving and enhancing the welfare of others), and tradition (whose goal is respect, commitment, and acceptance of the customs and ideas that one's culture or religion provides). From immigrant responses to the two life-review questions, we also identified the ethics that they think are important to pursue at some point in their lives, using the three cultural ethics of Shweder and his colleagues:[9] ethics of autonomy, community, and divinity. According to Shweder and his colleagues, community and divinity predominate in non-Western cultures.

For our second study (i.e., our pluralist study), we asked Protestant pastors, religious academics, and thought leaders in Brazil and China, "What are the major issues that the church is currently facing in society?" Interviews were carried out by the first author on any one of three trips to

---

7. Shalom Schwartz has developed and empirically validated cross-cultural measures of the values. His corpus of research is too extensive to cite here but groundbreaking in its contributions to our understanding of individual and cultural values. For a summary, see Schwartz, "Overview," 14.

8. Our methodology however follows that of Frimer and Walker, who build on the work of Emmons, *The Psychology of Ultimate Concerns*. Emmons asks people to name their current goals or strivings, which may be personal, spiritual, work-related, or global. Strivings express one's underlying motivations and can give direction and weight to the expression of these motivations. By identifying the Schwartz values in these strivings, we approximate the person's underlying constructions, described in this study as relevances. This technique for describing a person's values is less direct than the technique favored by Schwartz (i.e., asking individuals to rate each of the values individually) but has been successfully pioneered in recent research by Jeremy Frimer and Lawrence Walker, "Reconciling." Two coders separately analyzed the strivings following the coding manual of Jeremy Frimer and Lawrence Walker ("VEiN Relationship Coding Manual") and in the process developed a more extensive coding manual for strivings (available from the first author).

9. Shweder et al., "The 'Big Three' of Morality," 138.

Brazil. Two colleagues accompanied the first author on the first trip, Dr. Ruth Melkonian-Hoover and Dr. Sharon Ketcham. Interviews took one to two hours to conduct, were transcribed verbatim, and were analyzed for constructions that describe an issue given in response to this question. These constructions were generally phrases (although on rare occasions paragraphs) and roughly approximate (we argue) the complex Schutzian concept of "relevance structures." Only one Chinese interview is available and that interview took place in the United States because of concerns about safety for religious pastors and academics in mainland China. Translators were present for both the values study and the pluralist study, as needed.

We chose Brazil and China because of their economic promise, which both countries continue to offer, despite broad cultural and economic challenges in recent years. For the values study, we interviewed religious immigrants from Brazil and China, all of whom lived in the northeastern United States at the time our research took place. For the pluralist study, interviews with pastors, academics, and thought leaders took place in Brazil (with one exception of a Chinese academic and pastor who was interviewed in the northeastern United States). These participants represent countries that were earlier designated as BRIC countries[10] (i.e., Brazil, Russia, India, and China)—nations that were at similar stages of economic development and expected to become larger forces in the world economy.

We also chose to focus on Brazil and China because of recent significant religious growth. The number of Protestant Christians in Brazil and China has more than doubled over the past four decades. Brazil has the largest community of Catholics and the second largest community of Protestants and Pentecostals in the world.[11] It is a region of high religious belief, moderate religious practice, and traditional values.[12] In 2010, about 91 percent of Brazilians reported believing in God. Approximately 76 percent of Brazilians were Catholics who may be largely non-practicing, and 28 percent were Protestants who were largely Pentecostals and generally religiously active. In research by Johnson and Zurlo, 13 percent reported that they are dually affiliated—i.e., belong to more than one category of believers, one of which was often Catholic and the other, Protestant.[13] The

---

10. O'Neill, "Building Better Global Economic BRICs."

11. Johnson and Ross, eds., *Atlas of Global Christianity*, 89, 93, 101.

12. Inglehart and Carballo, "Does Latin America Exist?," 34–47; Freston, "Religious Change," 2.

13. Freston, "Religious Change"; Johnson and Zurlo, eds., *World Christian Database*.

number of Catholics has been declining, but Protestants have more than doubled since 1970, primarily due to growth among Pentecostals. This growth is predicted to stabilize soon, and Protestants are expected to remain highly diversified, comprising many denominations.[14]

The two major divisions among Protestants in Brazil are the Pentecostals, who make up roughly 82 percent of the membership of Protestant churches in Brazil, and the "mission" or historic churches, among which the Presbyterians and Baptists are the largest denominations.[15] All these groups—Pentecostals, Presbyterians, and Baptists—were represented in our immigrant group and in our group of pastors and academics, and many of the lay people in particular were relatively recent converts from Catholicism.

Christians in China are more difficult to count but their numbers are nevertheless also on the increase. An estimated 8.1 percent of Chinese nationals are Christians, and they constitute the fastest growing religious population in the country. Most are Protestant; roughly 7.4 percent of Chinese nationals report that they are affiliated with an independent or Protestant Christian group, and 1.1 percent report that they are Roman Catholic. These percentages add up to more than the estimated 8.1 percent because some individuals report more than one affiliation (.5 percent).[16] In comparison, Christians comprised less than 1 percent of the population in the 1970 census, taken during Mao Zedong's regime when religion in China was severely restricted and Christian leaders were purged. China's current constitution (adopted in 1982) legally protects the rights of religious institutions, but in practice the state-sponsored Three-Self Church has historically been more protected than the unregistered churches, often called "family" or "house" churches, which have no protections.[17]

The Chinese church faces political issues, but it also faces a broad array of other challenges because it is growing, urbanizing, and

---

In comparison, the Brazilian Institute for Geography and Statistics (IBGE) reports 65 percent Catholic, 22 percent Protestant, and 8 percent nonreligious.

14. Freston, "Brazil," 298.

15. Novais, "All about Religions in Brazil"; Johnson and Zurlo, *World Christian Database*.

16. Yang, *Religion in China*, 83; Johnson and Zurlo, *World Christian Database*. The Pew Research Center's "Global Christianity" places the number of Christians at about 5 percent in 2010.

17. Fulton, *China's Urban Christians*, 10–11, 126–34.

professionalizing.[18] According to the China Religion Survey 2015, released by the National Survey Research Center (NSRC) at Renmin University in Beijing, religious believers are younger than ever; religious clergy are better educated than ever; and Protestant churches are more indigenous than ever, with 82 percent of Protestant churches, registered and unregistered, having distinctive Chinese characteristics. Indeed, even though change appears to be the norm for modernizing cultures, it may be even more characteristic of Chinese than Brazilian Christianity.

Values Study

Values have historically been identified as central features of cultures.[19] In this project, 48 individuals—12 Brazilian Protestants and 12 Brazilian Catholics, 12 Chinese Protestants and 12 Chinese Catholics—were identified by their pastors or priests as religious exemplars. Participants were highly religious,[20] except for one participant. Despite being identified by his priest as a religious exemplar, this Chinese Catholic reported not being a Christian.[21]

Immigrants were interviewed to assess whether members of these subcultures continue to hold values that reflect their country of origin. Following Schwartz,[22] we measured ten values including tradition, benevolence, and stimulation (as defined above). Additionally values measured were: security (whose goal is safety, harmony, and stability in society, relationships, and the self), conformity (whose goal is restraint of actions and impulses that are likely to upset or harm others and violate social expectations or norms), universalism (whose goal is understanding, appreciating, tolerating, and protecting the welfare of all people and of nature), equality (whose goal is equal opportunity for all), power (whose goal is social status and prestige, or control over people and resources), self-direction (whose

---

18. Fulton, *China's Urban Christians*.

19. Inglehart and Carballo, "Does Latin America Exist?," 34; Schwartz, "Overview," 14; Weber, *The Protestant Ethic*.

20. Religion was "very important" to 80 percent of the participants, 98 percent reported that they were "moderately to extremely" interested in religion, and 71 percent reported attending church at least once a week.

21. Brazilian participants had been in the U.S. a mean of 13 years (range 2-26) and Chinese participants, 16 years (range 2-40).

22. Schwartz, "Rethinking Concept and Measurement," 5-13; Schwartz, "Culture Matters," 6-9.

goal is independent thought and action), and hedonism (whose goal is pleasure or sensuous gratification for the self).

Schwartz[23] derived seven basic cultural orientations (or value-types) which map onto these values, of which three are of specific interest to us: North American, Confucian-influenced, and Latin American regions. These regions were described by their location on three bipolar cultural value dimensions: egalitarianism versus hierarchy (which incorporates the values of power, equality, and conformity), autonomy versus embeddedness (which incorporates benevolence, tradition, security, stimulation, self-direction, and hedonism), and mastery versus harmony (which incorporates universalism). The Confucian-influenced region that includes China is characterized by a heavy emphasis on hierarchy and mastery, high levels of communal embeddedness, and a rejection of egalitarianism and harmony. The Latin American region is characterized by lower levels of hierarchy and embeddedness than in Asian cultures, but higher levels of intellectual autonomy. In comparison to the Latin American region, North Americans are higher on hierarchy, mastery, and autonomy, and lower on harmony and egalitarianism. A more specifically "Catholic" cluster within the Latin American region is marked by significant emphases on traditional values such as conformity and security.[24] The same values were measured in our participants as in this earlier research by Schwartz, and these cultural patterns potentially distinguish our participants.

Individual values are also meaningful; immigrants who are religious are likely to favor certain values.[25] Earlier research indicates that religious people tend to attribute high importance to values that reflect conservation, i.e., tradition, security, and conformity. They attribute lower importance to values of self-transcendence; that is, they value benevolence but not universalism. Finally, religious people generally attribute low importance to values indicating openness to change and self-enhancement such as stimulation, self-direction, and hedonism.

Individuals organize their values into an ethic—or a systematic structure of interrelationships among beliefs and values.[26] Persons make

---

23. Schwartz, "A Theory of Cultural Value Orientations."

24. Inglehart and Carballo, "Does Latin America Exist?," 41.

25. Roccas and Elster, "Values and Religiosity," 193–212; Saraglou et al. "Values and Religiosity," 721–34.

26. Arnett et al., "Ideological Views," 69; Shweder et al., "The 'Big Three' of Morality," 138.

meaning by developing an "ideological system" or "coherent body of shared images, ideas, and ideals which . . . provides for the participants a coherent, if systematically simplified, over-all orientation in space and time, in means and ends."[27]

Three distinct but coherent "clusters" of moral concerns or ethical systems have been described in earlier research that characterize people of diverse cultures—the "Big Three" of morality. The ethic of autonomy relies on such regulatory concepts as harm, rights, and justice, and emphasizes an individual's right to self-interest and non-interference; the ethic of community is based on such moral concepts as duty, hierarchy, and interdependency, which together aim to protect the moral integrity of the society or community; and the ethic of divinity is derived from concepts about sacred or natural order, tradition, sanctity, sin, and pollution. Central to the ethic of divinity is a conceptualization of the self as a "spiritual entity connected to some sacred or natural order of things and as a responsible bearer of a legacy that is elevated and divine."[28]

The research reported here is an initial attempt to explore whether the concept of the "stranger's address" continues to hold, even if to a lesser degree than in traditional cultures, despite pressures toward pluralism. Earlier research[29] predicted that our Chinese participants, as members of a Confucian culture, would favor egalitarianism, mastery, and hierarchy more than Brazilians, who are members of a Latin American culture. To the degree that both have been acculturated into the United States, both would be expected to mention values for affective autonomy (e.g., stimulation, hedonism) more often and for embeddedness (e.g., security, tradition, benevolence, conformity) less often when compared to native populations in these cultures.

Describing our participant values is complex. Brazilians favored achievement and self-direction more than Chinese, making them more agentic (or able to make the decision to act) and less communal in their immediate goals. Both Brazilians and Chinese individuals mentioned universalism, conformity, and security less often, as predicted, but benevolence was mentioned more often and stimulation less often than expected, perhaps reflecting their Christian beliefs. Finally, divinity was the dominant

27. Erikson, *Identity*, 189–90.
28. Shweder et al., "The 'Big Three' of Morality," 138.
29. Schwartz, "Rethinking Concept and Measurement," 5–13; Schwartz, "A Theory of Cultural Value Orientations;" Schwartz, "Culture Matters," 6–9.

ethic, but in a surprise outcome, Chinese favored autonomy and Brazilians favored community.

These cultural values are expressed along with religious values, although our participants did not consistently show the religious values as expected. Earlier research indicated that religious individuals favor conservation over universalism, stimulation, self-direction, and hedonism; however, our participants mentioned self-direction more frequently, and conformity and security less frequently than expected, although hedonism and stimulation were also less frequently mentioned. Further, although our Catholic participants were expected to favor the values of tradition, conformity, and security more than Protestants, these two groups did not differ in their values, perhaps in part because the Brazilian immigrants had been raised in a Catholic country.

Differences between the values of Brazilians and Chinese, documented here, suggest that participants retain elements of their "address" (i.e., echoes of their origins). Their beliefs are, however, shaped by multiple influences, including the cultures that they come to inhabit, and their religiousness. Pluralism thus undermines the coherence of beliefs from one's birth address, as Berger argues. These Brazilian and Chinese immigrants, in the United States for more than a decade on average, retained the values and ethics of their homeland, with Brazilians particularly favoring immediate success (as measured by goals) but long-term communalism (as measured by their ethics). The Chinese, from a more ambiguously communalist society,[30] favored autonomy. Both groups also showed American values (e.g., low levels of universalism and conformity) and religious values (e.g., high levels of benevolence and an ethic of divinity), demonstrating that their values originate from a plurality of sources.

Perhaps because experiences are so individual, we should be surprised at *any* uniformity of values at all in our participants. Nevertheless, we found significant consistency by culture and religion. In these findings, we document yet another instance of Berger's social constructionism when we note that individuals carry their religious and cultural histories with them into modernizing contexts; all of their experiences together form the stranger's values, grounded not in the particular address that someone is born into (as Berger described it) but in individualized experience.

---

30. Schwartz, "Beyond Individualism/Collectivism," 107.

Pluralist Ideas Study

In the second project, we sought to show that Berger's theory of "cognitive contamination" is evident in the conversations of individuals from modernizing countries. For these interviews, we asked an open-ended question: What are the major issues that the church (or your church) is currently facing in society right now? We carried out fifteen interviews with thirty-two academics, pastors, and thought leaders in Brazil and one Chinese pastor/seminary professor in the Boston area who travels frequently to China. We transcribed the interviews, and then reviewed them for pluralism in ideas.

We operationalized pluralist ideas by coding the interviews for instances in which interviewees described pluralism in context (e.g., Christian churches from different denominations or within the same denomination coexisting with one another) or pluralism in ideas (i.e., two religious or religious/secular ideas that were presented by the participant as in juxtaposition). Almost all of the thought leaders and pastors talked about pluralism in ideas—in most cases by describing pluralism without using the word, citing the coexistence of ideas or belief systems as an issue for the church. A member of a group of seminary women,[31] when asked to describe the church scene in Brazil, described it as pluralist in these words: "Here you have the conservative church, the middle way church, and the fairly liberal church." Gedeon Alencar, a Pentecostal academic and pastor who has written extensively on the history and challenges of Pentecostalism, described the challenge of pluralism in terms of identity: "We have a universe that is extremely plural. One of the biggest questions for Pentecostals is the identity question. I call it the 'diffusion of identity.' We don't have direct precepts of what it means to be Pentecostal in theological, social, political terms, etc."[32] Pluralism in ideas can create challenges for pastors or, alternatively, opportunities for evangelism. Rev. Valdinei Ferreira, Independent Presbyterian Cathedral pastor, framed the challenge of pluralism in evangelistic terms: "The pastoral advice is to welcome and then teach the word of the gospel in a truthful manner, and the person will make their decision based on what the Holy Spirit leads. Some people will change their

---

31. FATIPI seminarians, interview by author, Dr. Sharon Ketcham, and Dr. Ruth Melkonian-Hoover, São Paulo, Brazil, August 10, 2015.

32. Gedeon de Alencar, interviews by author, São Paulo, Brazil, September 28, 2015, October 3, 2015. De Alencar has written several trenchant analyses of the church context in Brazil, particularly with focus on the Assemblies of God church but also more broadly. See *Matriz Pentecostal Brasileira* and *Protestantismo Tupiniquim*.

pattern of behavior and others will not be able to do that. Either they will accept it or fight it in their lives."[33]

Once pluralist ideas were identified, we distinguished among three kinds of social constructions. We coded *coexistence*, or the contextualization of beliefs or belief systems alongside other beliefs or belief systems; *conservation*, or efforts by individuals or groups to maintain the integrity of their traditional beliefs in a pluralist context; and *integration*, or evidence that the beliefs or constructions of individuals and groups have elements that contradict or transform earlier or core Christian beliefs, values, and constructions. Integration most directly captures Berger's construct of *cognitive contamination*.

COEXISTENCE. Coexistence refers to instances in which participants talked about two ideas or systems of ideas coinciding. These ideas or belief systems may consist of several different religious beliefs, or of religious beliefs in coexistence with secular beliefs. They may be internal within the same person or external between groups. For example, in a conversation with seminary women at Unicesumar in Maringá, Brazil,[34] one woman described another, saying that "Claudia[35] feels lost [in thinking about whether women should be ordained] because St. Paul [in the Bible] really does say that man is the head of the household." These internal conflicts were rarely expressed, however, perhaps because of the way the interview question was phrased (i.e., what are the issues in your church?).

Coexisting beliefs might also emerge within a church body, between faith groups, or with the government or society. Rev. Lisanias Moura, pastor of the Morumbi Baptist Church, said that the community group with which his church was organizing community events "started to prevent us from teaching the gospel, because they wanted to do a concert" in the same space. In describing the church's response to pressures to accept a gay and lesbian pastor, this same pastor said, "We are trying to learn to speak in a different way that is not extreme conservatism and excludes them from the church, but is not totally inclusive and accepting of their agenda."[36] Rev. Dr.

---

33. Valdinei Ferreira, interview by author, Dr. Sharon Ketcham, and Dr. Ruth Melkonian-Hoover, São Paulo, Brazil, August 10, 2015.

34. Unicesumar seminarians, interview by author and Dr. Ruth Melkonian-Hoover, August 13, 2015.

35. Name is changed to protect her identity.

36. Lisanias Moura, interview by author, September 27, 2015.

T. K. Chuang, the Chinese academic-pastor and sole Chinese participant, said that "the leaders, the ministers, they come from Taiwan. They are more serious biblically, theologically, and spiritually. But new members are often from China, so their world view, value system, everything is different."[37] In each case, these beliefs are in tension with one another but do not appear to be moving towards a clear resolution.

Individuals or groups with different belief systems may, however, coexist without conflict and even cooperatively work to achieve common goals. Rev. Lisanias talked about the difference between witnessing about God to the neighboring *favelado* (person who lives in the shacks in the low-income settlements generally on the city's edge) and the businessman in his office. In the first case, his approach is to talk about suffering; in the second, love. Dr. Wilson de Matos, President of Unicesumar, described the geographic distribution of Catholic and Protestant churches:[38] "Normally the Catholics are in the center of the city and the Protestants are outside." He described his own location as different, more complexly interwoven: "Here, they're all together. So they associate themselves and work together. Nobody has enough money or power to make all the decisions for everyone, so they have to work together to make solutions." Our Chinese academic, Rev. Dr. T. K. Chuang, attended prayer meetings convened by unregistered churches to which police were invited as representatives of the government, not as friends.

Finally, in our analysis of coexistence, we frequently heard stories of individuals with a desire to learn more about the church, because the church offers an alternative to societal values. This kind of pluralism can be summarized in the Christian phrase "love your neighbor" (Matt 22:39). For example, Marília de Camargo César, a journalist and author in São Paulo, described a person who said: "I need some help. I want to go to your church."[39] In this same interview, this journalist noted that "where I see more empowerment of women is in the NeoPentecostal churches, where women are ordained pastors as are their husbands." Her hope is that this empowerment can spread to other churches and the larger society. Helio

---

37. T. K. Chuang, interview by author, July 8, 2015.

38. Wilson de Matos, interview by author and Dr. Ruth Melkonian-Hoover, August 13, 14, 2015.

39. Marília de Camargo César, interview by author, Dr. Sharon Ketcham, and Dr. Ruth Melkonian-Hoover, August 10, 2015.

Nishimoto,[40] a Japanese-Brazilian man who is in the São Paolo Assembly, recognized that the church has political power for good, such that it might shape national laws that help to protect people or even move the nation toward greater acceptance of the place of Protestantism in society. In our analysis of coexisting ideas, we were particularly struck by these instances of the church's power to do good in a challenging context.

Even though we recorded our participants' perceptions of church issues at particular points in time, we realized by the way the beliefs were framed that they may be unstable and change over time. For example, two groups may be in conflict with each other, or a person may experience internal conflict over disparate ideas. This latter conflict is the everyday experience that psychologists call cognitive dissonance. Individuals who experience dissonance may seek some sort of resolution to resolve the internal conflict. Their efforts may lead them to reject intrusive beliefs, in a process we call conservation, or to integrate beliefs into a new synthesis, a process Berger calls "cognitive contamination." We now turn to these two types of social constructions.

CONSERVATION. Participants sometimes recognize challenges to their faith and resist them. In that case, they may make choices to maintain their existing belief system or, more actively, they may seek to reinforce and strengthen existing beliefs for self or others. Many comments that were coded "conservation" in these modernizing contexts are the statements of believers who wish to stay true to their belief system. They could have been made in any country in the world, whether modernizing or not: "We believe the Bible is the final authority. We are traditionalists." "Many stay very devoted and want to grow spiritually." "We believe that theology should be in every part of your life." These are the statements of believers who wish to stay true to their belief system.

These comments, made in response to questions about the issues for their church, were often followed by suggestions of ways to help people remain orthodox in their beliefs and even to take the added step of purifying the church and society. Rev. Valdinei recommends that pastors "teach the word of the gospel in a truthful manner";[41] Rev. Lisanias believes that "pastors not only need more theological training, but more examples of how to

---

40. Helio Nishimoto, interview by author, Dr. Sharon Ketcham, and Dr. Ruth Melkonian-Hoover, August 11, 2015.

41. Valdine Ferreira.

live the faith."[42] Marília, the Brazilian journalist, suggested that "[it would be useful] for churches to have an ethics code."[43] Rev. Dr. Mauro Meister, president of Andrew Jumper seminary at Mackenzie University, suggests that "Untrained pastors come to us and it's amazing; it's a big opportunity to influence them with serious theology and a reflection on ethics and moral issues, so they wouldn't reflect wrong on Christ."[44]

One church in Brazil, concerned about the maturity of its members, has self-consciously developed a strategy to help maintain personal integrity and develop Christian maturity. In this church, according to Marília, "the pastor has a professional Christian forum which is like a place of debate about professional issues. Many go to get more information. I see where I can look to improve the level of information."

INTEGRATION. In response to conflicts among beliefs, one may choose to resist and reject the new belief, as in conservation, or one may engage the belief, integrating it into one's belief system. Berger calls this *cognitive contamination* and defines it as the process by which the beliefs and values of others undermine the taken-for-granted status of one's own. He argues the centrality of this process for pluralism, and presents it as a challenge for believers. We recognize this process and measured it more broadly, calling it *integration*. We identified instances in which our participants described secularism or false belief mixed with core Christian beliefs (i.e., negative integration or contamination), and instances in which a new belief was thoughtfully integrated into the existing framework of beliefs without doing injustice to those beliefs or becoming less doctrinally correct (i.e., positive integration). We recognize that differentiating between positive and negative integration is problematic, and may differ depending on whose perspective is coded: the interviewer, the interviewee who is observing a third person, or the person being observed. Where possible, our coding reflects the interviewee's perspective.

"Brazilian culture is able to swallow up contradictions, bring them into their culture, and morph them into something that works!" So Gedeon Alencar describes the syncretistic character of Brazil. Thirteen of our fifteen participants gave examples of integration (whether positive or negative) as

42. Lisanias Moura.

43. Marília de Camargo César.

44. Mauro Meister, interview by author, Dr. Sharon Ketcham, and Dr. Ruth Melkonian-Hoover, August 10, 2015.

a church issue. The most common contaminants were prosperity theology, consumerism, and weak theology. Pastors who had been "contaminated" were described as being egotistical, materialist, or power hungry. We also heard about the sin of pride among pastors who were unwilling to work with others. To quote Rev. Lisanias, the leaders of churches who were unwilling to join a network of churches "tried to do things by themselves, as though they have the king in their stomachs, as though they are self-sufficient."[45]

From the instances that were identified, we heard multiple expressions of the ways in which cultural developments have challenged and changed faith, particularly with respect to consumerism and the prosperity gospel. At times, descriptions of contaminations were accompanied by lamentations for the cost this brings to the core beliefs of faith. Marília, who has written extensively about these issues, reports, "A lot of people . . . learn to believe in a different God and learn how to bargain with God as if God were a pagan idol."[46] Even when challenged with more defensible beliefs, some may find it hard to distinguish orthodoxy from misleading ideas. At a later point in the interview, Marília says, "One of the members of [a particular] church was asked, 'Can't you see they are stealing money from all of the members?' He responded, 'No, they are my friends.'" This contamination of ideas can perhaps be avoided by education: "If people cannot read properly, how can they discern that what the pastor is saying is rubbish?" asks Marília. As Berger suggests, individuals can and do change the beliefs of one another when these beliefs come in contact, undermining the certainty and orthodoxy of belief.

Positive integration—transformation of beliefs without contamination from false ideas—also occurred. Marília described the process of evangelism in this way: "They [Christians] influence society like little ants."[47] By moving out into the larger society with their message of the gospel in large numbers rather than with loud voices, believers are able to convert others to the faith. Rev. Lisanias relates his own conversion from simplistic to more complex thinking in these words: "Is there a space for feelings? We are so black and white, but God broke my heart and brought me to him."[48] Rev. Lisanias already knew God and his calling as a pastor, but learned something unexpected about God by being open to God when he was

45. Lisanias Moura.
46. Marília de Camargo César.
47. Ibid.
48. Lisanias Moura.

facing a tremendous challenge that he could not resolve on his own. Pastor Ricardo Chen, president of a seminary in São Paulo, said, "It's a beautiful thing, seeing transformation happening in their lives."[49] These seminarians were already believers but their experience of a seminary education that challenged them to act on their faith by serving others, while being supported cognitively and emotionally themselves, changed their lives and deepened their faith. Rev. Mauro Meister, another seminary president and pastor, says, "We receive a lot of people. They get tired of the prosperity gospel and, if they're coherent, they will search for something more stable and more grounded."[50] Rev. Meister recognized the difficulties of trying to help someone know God as Redeemer and Savior, when the person has only known God as a cosmic cash register. This ministry, when successful, results in positive transformation toward greater coherence in Christian beliefs.

Conclusion

What, then, is the stranger's address? How fluid is religious belief in the context of modernity? We explored the stranger's address as derived from the values and ethics of Brazilian and Chinese immigrants, wondering whether participants retain markers of their traditional culture, and found that these immigrants do retain such markers, but mixed in with markers from their contemporary culture and their religious beliefs. We did not find the degree of coherent beliefs that one would expect to find in traditional cultures, which would have allowed us to know what someone believed if we knew their country of origin. This identity no longer exists, as Berger notes—and values are somewhat fluid indeed.

Given the unique nature of each individual's "relevance structures" and the influence of modernity, it is perhaps surprising that, as a result of the values study, we were able to document shared beliefs among Protestants in comparison to Catholics, and among Brazilians in comparison to Chinese immigrants. Their shared beliefs attest to the cohesiveness of community and the durability of values, in some cases despite transitioning to a different culture and spending many years in the United States. We

---

49. Ricardo Chen, interview by author, Dr. Sharon Ketcham, and Dr. Ruth Melkonian-Hoover, August 12, 2015.

50. Mauro Meister.

The Stranger's Address in Modernizing Cultures

are products of our past and present, manifesting faith and culture in both individual and shared ways.

As we were able to document in the second study, Berger's marker of modernity—pluralism—is present in the voices of believers in modernizing societies. Our analysis of conversations about church issues with pastors, academics, and thought leaders in Brazil and China revealed multiple instances of pluralist ideas. In some cases, these ideas coexisted with one another, without rejection or integration. In other cases, however, expressions reflected efforts to conserve the integrity of one's beliefs in the face of challenge, or to integrate new and even contrasting beliefs into one's belief system. When positively framed, we came to see the process of integration as the essence of evangelism, described by the Brazilian journalist[51] as "they influence society like little ants" and by the Chinese academic as "pastors preach on that, step by step, part by part."

Despite worries that pluralism undermines faith, in these two countries at least, the modernizing process has been accompanied by rapid growth in evangelicalism, perhaps undermining core Christian beliefs, but also permitting explosive growth among believers. Several problems accompany this growth, problems that have been identified by our participants, including expressions of Pentecostal identity that are not solidly Biblical (perhaps in part because Pentecostal theology is minimalist), emergence of false beliefs (e.g., prosperity theology), and proliferation of denominations, leading to problems with unity in the church context. Nevertheless, pluralism, far from undermining Christianity, has allowed the number of Protestant believers to at least double in each of these cultural contexts over the past few decades.

Berger agrees that "pluralism benefits faith." His argument hinges on the idea that faith, at least for evangelicals, is a choice and not a birthright. It is true that exercising choice to believe may mean that individuals choose *not* to believe, a detriment to faith. It is also true, and here we concur with Berger's optimism, that we are called to make a choice to serve God. This choice then becomes central to our social construction of faith, which leaves us short of knowing God in his fullness (a goal we seek but can never wholly achieve) but nevertheless allows us to approach (or approximate) knowing who he is.

Serving God is a calling and a responsibility. The loss of certainty Berger claims is endemic to modernity, and which he concludes is good

51. Marília de Camargo César.

for faith is, in fact, a core Christian belief, part and parcel of the Christian experience. The writer of Hebrews tells us (Hebrews 11:1, NIV) that "faith is confidence in what we hope for and assurance about what we do not see." This "leap of faith" is not certainty, and the certainty that some believe can be found in the church is not as certain as it seems. By these words, we do not mean to undermine the possibility of profound religious experiences or of knowing God, only to recognize our human engagement in the process.

We concur that pluralism changes faith in significant and observable ways. Faith becomes more personal, transformed by modernizing forces outside of the individual. In that sense, to again quote Berger, "pluralism deepens the question of what I myself—and not just some abstract community to which I am supposed to belong—*really* believe."

Berger's pluralist theory[52] successfully challenges secularization theory, according to the authors in this volume and others in the larger academy. In that debate, the resilience of faith in contrast to secularization is particularly noteworthy. The markers of modernity, culturally described by Berger, also appear in everyday conversations about faith, as documented in this chapter. Cognitive contamination may be met with efforts to maintain integrity; contextualization may lead to evangelism. In the challenges of daily life, participants must derive their own coherent beliefs and seek personal integrity. With the techniques of constructivist psychology, as academics, we can capture the sociological mechanisms that Berger identifies. As persons, we can celebrate with the individuals who engage modernity and emerge with their faith transformed but made stronger and more personal. This is the message of pluralist theory: Modernity challenges individuals to know what they believe despite being surrounded by a cacophony of voices. It is in this sense that, for Christians, pluralism is indeed good for you!

Bibliography

Alencar, Gedeon Freire de. *Matriz Pentecostal Brasileira: Assembleias de Deus 1911–2011*. Rio de Janeiro, Brazil: Editora Novas Diálogos, 2013.

———. *Protestantismo Tupiniquim: Hipóteses sobre a (não) contribuição evangélica à cultura Brasileira*. 3rd ed. São Paulo, Brazil: Arte Editorial, 2005.

---

52. In the book *Many Altars*, Berger describes his version of pluralist theory. This version is not without critics, as chapters in this volume indicate. Nevertheless, Berger and others struggle to describe forces of modernity that are very real and that impact the daily lives of Christian believers. They deserve our attention.

Arnett, Jeffrey J., et al. "Ideological Views in Emerging Adulthood: Balancing Autonomy and Community." *Journal of Adult Development* 8 (2001) 69–79.

Berger, Peter L. *The Many Altars of Modernity: Toward a Paradigm for Religion in a Pluralist Age*. Boston: De Gruyter, 2014.

Berger, Peter L., and Luckmann, Thomas. *The Social Construction of Reality: A Treatise in the Sociology of Knowledge*. Garden City, NY: Anchor, 1966.

Brazilian Institute for Geography and Statistics (IBGE). 2010 Census. https://ww2.ibge.gov.br/english/estatistica/populacao/censo2010/default.shtm.

China Religion Survey 2015. National Survey Research Center (NSRC), Remnin University. http://crs.ruc.edu.cn.

Cook, Kaye V., et al. "Religiousness and Spirituality among Highly Religious Emerging Adults." *Journal of Psychology and Christianity* 34 (2015) 250–63.

Cook, Kaye V., et al. "Folk Conceptions of Virtue among Cambodian American Buddhists and Christians: A Hermeneutic Analysis." *Psychology of Religion and Spirituality* 2.2 (2010) 83–103.

Crossley, Michele L. "Formulating Narrative Psychology: The Limitations of Contemporary Social Constructionism." *Narrative Inquiry* 13 (2003) 287–300.

Emmons, Robert A. *The Psychology of Ultimate Concerns: Motivation and Spirituality in Personality*. New York: Guilford, 1999.

Erikson, Erik. *Identity: Youth and Crisis*. New York: Norton, 1968.

Freston, Paul. "Brazil." In *Encyclopedia of Protestantism*, vol. 1, edited by Hans Hillerbrand, 294–8. New York: Routledge, 2003.

———. "Religious Change and Economic Development in Latin America." Paper presented at the Conference on Religion and Development, Vrije Universiteit Amsterdam, June 2007. http://www.religionanddevelopment.nl.

Frimer, Jeremy A., and Lawrence J. Walker. "Reconciling the Self and Morality: An Empirical Model of Moral Centrality Development." *Developmental Psychology* 45 (2009) 1669–81.

———. "*VEiN Relationship Coding Manual.*" Unpublished manuscript, Department of Psychology, University of British Columbia, Vancouver, BC, 2010.

Fulton, Brent. *China's Urban Christians: A Light That Cannot Be Hidden*. Eugene, OR: Pickwick, 2015.

Inglehart, Ronald, and Marita Carballo. "Does Latin America Exist? (And Is There a Confucian Culture?): A Global Analysis of Cross-Cultural Differences." *PS, Political Science and Politics* 30 (1997) 34–47.

Johnson, Todd, and Kenneth Ross, eds. *Atlas of Global Christianity*. Edinburgh, UK: Edinburgh University Press, 2009.

Johnson, Todd, and Gina Zurlo, eds. *World Christian Database*. Center For the Study of Global Christianity at Gordon-Conwell Theological Seminary. Boston: Brill, 2007.

Jovchelovitch, Sandra, and Martin W. Bauer. "Narrative Interviewing." LSE Research Online, August 2007. http://eprints.lse.ac.uk/2633.

Novais, Andréa. "All about Religions in Brazil." Brazil Business, last modified 9 January 2013, http://thebrazilbusiness.com/article/all-about-religions-in-brazil.

O'Neill, Jim. "Building Better Global Economic BRICs." Goldman Sachs: Global Economics Paper no. 66, 30 November 2001. http://www.goldmansachs.com/our-thinking/archive/archive-pdfs/build-better-brics.pdf.

Pew Research Center. "Global Christianity: A Report on the Size and Distribution of the World's Christian Population." Forum on Religion & Public Life, 19 December 2011. http://www.pewforum.org/2011/12/19/global-christianity-exec.

Roccas, Sonia, and Elster, Andrey. "Values and Religiosity." In *Religion, Personality, and Social Behavior*, edited by Vassilis Saroglou, 193–212. New York: Psychology Press, 2014.

Sandage, Stephen J., et al. "Hermeneutics and Psychology: A Review and Dialectical Model." *Review of General Psychology* 12 (2008) 344–64.

Saraglou, Vassilis, et al. "Values and Religiosity: A Meta-analysis of Studies using Schwartz's Model." *Personality and Individual Differences* 37 (2004) 721–34.

Schutz, Alfred, and Thomas Luckmann. *The Structures of the Life-World*. Translated by Richard M. Zanere and H. Tristram Engelhardt. Evanston, IL: Northwestern University Press, 1973.

Schwartz, Shalom. "A Theory of Cultural Value Orientations: Explication and Applications." *Comparative Sociology* 5 (2006) 137–81.

———. "Beyond Individualism/Collectivism: New Cultural Dimensions of Values." In *Individualism and Collectivism: Theory, Method and Applications*, edited by Uichol Kim, et al., 85–119. Cross-Cultural Research and Methodology, vol. 18. Thousand Oaks, CA: Sage, 1994.

———. "Culture Matters: National Value Cultures, Sources and Consequences." In *Understanding Culture: Theory, Research and Application*, edited by Chi-Yue Chiu,et al., 127–50. New York: Psychology Press, 2009. https://www.researchgate.net/publication/274138930_Culture_matters_National_value_cultures_sources_and_consequences.

———. "An Overview of the Schwartz Theory of Basic Values." *Online Readings in Psychology and Culture* 2 (2012) 1–20. http://scholarworks.gvsu.edu/cgi/viewcontent.cgi?article=1116&context=orpc.

———. "Rethinking the Concept and Measurement of Societal Culture in Light of Empirical Findings." *Journal of Cross-Cultural Psychology* 45 (2014) 5–13.

Shweder, Richard A., et al. "The 'Big Three' of Morality (Autonomy, Community, Divinity), and the 'Big Three' Explanations of Suffering." In *Morality and Health*, edited by Allan Brandt and Paul Rozin, 119–69. New York: Routledge, 1997.

Smith, C. R., and M. L. Denton. *Soul Searching: The Religious and Spiritual Lives of American Teenagers*. New York: Oxford University Press, 2005.

Smith, C. R., and P. Snell. *Souls in Transition: The Religious and Spiritual Lives of Emerging Adults*. New York: Oxford University Press, 2009.

Tashakkori, Abbas, et al. "Utilizing Mixed Methods in Psychological Research." In *Research Methods in Psychology*, 2nd ed., edited by Irving B. Weiner, John A. Schinka, and Wayne F. Velicer, 428–50. Handbook of Psychology, vol. 2. Hoboken, NJ: Wiley, 2012.

Weber, Max. *The Protestant Ethic and the Spirit of Capitalism*. Los Angeles: Roxbury, 2002.

Yang, Fenggang. *Religion in China: Survival and Revival under Communist Rule*. New York: Oxford University Press, 2012.

Name/Subject Index

Alfred Schutz, 6, 7, 10
   Schutzian, 7, 116
Anabaptist(s), 29, 30, 31
apostle(s), 3, 66
   Apostle Paul, 1, 7, 9
   Apostle Thomas, 70
   Jude the Apostle, 73
atheist(s), 4, 5, 56, 66
atheism, 5, 14, 21, 56
   methodological atheism, 5, 35, 48
Baptist(s), 29, 31, 33, 106, 117, 123
Bharatiya Janata Party (BJP), 64–65, 68–76
Buddhist, 3, 4, 64
   Buddhism, 3, 15
Calvinist(s), 5, 6
Catholic(s), 2, 5, 7, 12, 15, 48–9, 54, 58–60, 72, 90–91, 98, 102, 116–19, 121, 124, 128
   Catholicism, 49, 75, 90, 117
   Roman Catholic Church, 6, 12, 16
Christian sociology, 4, 17–20, 23–28, 48
coexistence, 54, 72, 114, 122–24
cognitive contamination, 1, 113–14, 122–26, 130
cognitive bargaining, 12, 50
complementarian(s), 96
confessional pluralism, 51–52, 55–57, 60
conservation, 119, 121, 123, 125–26
core of faith (including core values, core beliefs), 9, 12–13, 40–41, 43, 50–54, 57, 63, 123, 126–27, 129–30

desecularization, 62
dialogue (including religious and interreligious dialogue), 12, 14–16, 44
ecumenical, 15–6
egalitarian, 92, 96, 106–7, 119–20
Evangelicals, 91, 97, 103–6, 129
feminist/feminism, 79, 80–82, 86–88, 92, 102, 107, 109
forgiveness, 80, 82–88
formulas for (of) peace, 6
fundamentalism, 3, 9, 18, 20, 51, 63
globalization, 1, 3
Herman Dooyeweerd, 23–24
Hindu(s), 1, 14, 52, 63–74, 76
   Hinduism, 14–15, 65–66, 72–73
   Hindutva (Hindu nationalism), 63–70, 73–5
Hugo Grotius, 5, 30, 39, 41–42, 48–49
Integration, 123, 126–27, 129
Jews, 1, 2, 6, 7, 11, 13, 15, 50–2, 55, 72
Judaism, 13, 50
liberalism, 43, 50, 107
   political liberalism, 39
Lutheran(s), 6, 11, 51
   Lutheranism, 4
Many Altars of Modernity, 4, 29–30, 34, 38, 46, 62, 63, 76
marginalization, 50–51, 53, 91, 95, 97, 109
Martin Luther, 6, 9–11
   Martin Luther King, Jr., 85, 105
Marxism, 25, 50
Max Weber, 11, 21
   Weberian, 25

Name/Subject Index

modernity, 1, 3–5, 12, 38, 62, 64, 76, 92, 101, 105–6, 108–9, 114, 128–30
natural law, 6, 33–35, 49
orthodox, 1–2, 5, 13–14, 16, 41, 92, 125
    orthodoxy, 1, 22, 127
Pentecostal gender bargain, 92, 109
Pentecostalism, 3, 91, 100, 108, 122
pluralist/pluralism, 1, 4–9, 11–12, 14–16, 18–19, 25, 29–31, 34–35, 37–47, 51–57, 59–64, 75–76, 79, 88, 90–92, 95, 103, 105, 109, 112, 114–16, 120–24, 126, 129–30
    principled pluralism, 46, 55, 57
Pope (including Francis I, John XXIII, Pius IX, Benedict XVI), 4, 7, 12, 30, 32, 34
Presbyterian, 104, 117, 122
prosperity gospel, 127–28
Protestant(s), 2, 5–6, 9, 30, 48–49, 58–9, 65, 98, 101, 115–18, 121, 124, 128–29
    Protestantism, 5, 49, 98, 101, 125
Reformation, 5, 9, 48, 95, 104–5

Reformed, 6
relevance structures, 7, 79, 88, 114, 116, 128
religious pluralism, 4, 12, 14, 40, 51–52, 62–64
rumors of angels, *A Rumor of Angels*, 21
sectarian, nonsectarian, 58–60
secular discourse, 4–5, 30–31, 34–35, 41–42, 109
secular space(s), 5–6, 29, 40, 42, 47–53, 60, 112
secularity, 4–5, 18–19, 30–35, 38, 40, 44, 47–48, 52–53
    secularism, 5, 40, 43, 47–51, 64, 126
secularization theory, 4, 18, 25, 42, 46, 51–54, 61–62, 130
sola fide, 9, 10, 41
sphere sovereignty, 6
stranger's address, the, 2, 113, 120, 128
structural pluralism, 55, 56, 57, 60
Vatican (including I and II), 12, 15, 74

Scripture Index

Matthew
5:45   56
13:24–30   36–43, 56
22:39   124

John
1:1–4   49

Romans
13   42
3:28   9

1 Corinthians
15:14   13

2 Corinthians
10:5   22

Colossians
1:15–20   49
1:17   22

Hebrews
1:1–3   49
11:1   10, 130

www.ingramcontent.com/pod-product-compliance
Lightning Source LLC
Chambersburg PA
CBHW031500160426
43195CB00010BB/1051